# SMALLER CHURCH YOUTH MINISTRY

## NO STAFF
## NO MONEY
## NO PROBLEM!

D1474252

BRAD FISCUS WITH STEPHANIE CARO

FOREWORD BY DUFFY ROBBINS

## SMALLER CHURCH YOUTH MINISTRY:
## NO STAFF, NO MONEY, NO PROBLEM

Copyright © 2016 by Abingdon Press

All rights reserved.

ISBN: 9781501825811

16 17 18 19 20 21 22 23 24 25—10 9 8 7 6 5 4 3 2 1

MANUFACTURED IN THE UNITED STATES OF AMERICA

# CONTENTS

# DEDICATION

To my mom and dad,

Thank you for revealing Jesus Christ to me daily.

Your love is the best inheritance I could ever receive.

Love, Brad

# FOREWORD

## THE POWER OF SMALL MULTIPLIED BY THE POWER OF GOD

The small group of young people meeting alone on an August afternoon in the shade of a patch of trees near Sloan's Meadow along Massachusetts' Hoosac River probably wouldn't have registered so much as a burp on anyone's Youth Ministry Richter Scale. The numbers certainly weren't impressive; the program was pretty stripped-down. And they had to change locations right in the middle of the meeting because of a thunderstorm. In fact, they literally ended up meeting in a pile of hay where they basically waited out the rain by praying together. But that small group of young people believed in a big God, and they prayed that summer afternoon that God might somehow use the five of them to communicate the gospel to those around the world "who were not Christians."

Looking back on it now, it probably wouldn't have fit anyone's idea of a youth ministry success story. But in that simple gathering—now known as "The Haystack Prayer Meeting"—God began a work that has impacted thousands and probably millions of lives around the world. In fact, within six years of that Saturday afternoon in 1806, that small group of young people had helped to launch the American Board of Commissioners for Foreign Missions (ABCFM), and, through their collective efforts, some of the very first American Protestant missionaries set out for foreign shores. Today, some two hundred-plus years later, the ABCFM has sent out nearly 5,000 missionaries to thirty-four different fields. And it all started with a very big God and a very small group of young people. (See *Global Ministries*, 28 February 2006.)

That's why this book you hold in your hands offers such a compelling vision. Brad and Stephanie believe that God can do bigger things in a smaller church than we often dare to hope or believe.

## THE POWER OF SMALL

In one of my first writing assignments, I was asked to write curriculum for The United Methodist Church, specifically curriculum that could be used on Sunday nights for United Methodist Youth Fellowship. After submitting my first few lessons, I received some coaching from my editor. He noted that one of my learning activities had centered around the students building a Human Pyramid (that is, students stacked on top of each other, five on the bottom, then four, then three, and so on). He politely went on to explain that the average United Methodist youth group had an average attendance of precisely six kids, and that he wasn't confident that the "pyramid idea will be very effective with only three or four young people." It struck me as a reasonable concern. I tried to imagine three kids excitedly building a pyramid, one on top of two ... and stopping there. Admittedly, it didn't sound very engaging. So I thanked him for his guidance, reworked the pyramid activity, and removed the relay race from lesson five.

What that little exercise forced me to see was this: yes, size does matter when it comes to programming and planning, and there are some real limitations faced by smaller youth groups. But it also stretched me to conclude: no, that doesn't mean God is somehow limited by a smaller church. The cook who is limited by the lack of ingredients just has to come up with new recipes. As long as there's fire to cook with, and salt for flavor (for the full recipe see

Matthew 3:11 and Matthew 5:13), there's still lots of potential for people to be fed. It was in coming up with those new recipes that I began to see some real advantages in a smaller youth group. That's when I became a believer in the power of small.

This isn't a new idea, of course. Theologian Robert Capon in his study of the parables of Jesus observed that the five primary images Jesus used for the kingdom of God are "The Little, The Lost, The Least, The Last and The Dead." Jesus understood that even a few loaves and fish could feed a multitude, and that even faith the size of a mustard seed could move mountains. Little wonder that although Jesus had multitudes of followers, he chose to spend the bulk of his time with a small group of twelve. We can imagine Jesus might have agreed with that old Ethiopian proverb that says: "With enough patience and saliva, even an ant can swallow an elephant!"

But, before you go any further in this book, just to be clear, let's affirm three clear advantages of a smaller youth group.

## 1. Intimacy

I heard a story about a very well-known youth worker who was surprised at a conference by a young woman who thanked him for the impact he had made in her life.

"You are the reason I met Jesus," she said.

And so he asked, "What was it? Was it a talk? Was it our group? Did you hear me speak on a retreat?"

"No," she replied, "You remembered my name."

Every teenager wants to be known. We all do. And it's just a fact: the smaller the youth group, the greater is the opportunity to really know each student and minister to them as an individual. Jesus said, "I am the good shepherd; I know my sheep and my sheep know me" (John 10:14, NIV). This is Shepherding 101: if you have a smaller flock, you have a better chance of knowing each of the

SMALLER CHURCH YOUTH MINISTRY

sheep. Think about it this way: when large youth groups gather, one of the first things they do is divide all the students into small groups. So, if you have a smaller youth group, God has just saved you a step!

## 2. Involvement

You've probably heard this little aphorism: The church is like a football game. There is a small number of people on the field who don't really need the exercise, but they're the ones in the game. And there are large numbers of people in the stands who desperately need the exercise, but they often never make it out onto the field. If you have a small group, it's a lot easier to get all of the kids into the game.

Perhaps you've seen this principle at work. Let's say, for example, you go Christmas caroling with a large youth group. You've got three people actually singing on the porch, twenty-three kids watching from the lawn, two kids who stayed in the van, and one person throwing snow on the guy next to him. It's just tough to keep everybody involved. With a smaller youth group, you have a better chance of turning spectators into participators.

## 3. Innovation

Max Weber, in his study of organizations, found that the larger the organization the more likely it was to turn in on itself and begin to serve its own needs instead of the needs of its constituents. Unfortunately, we often see this played out in youth ministry.

As groups get larger, they tend to require more infrastructure and maintenance. They start to play it safer. They become less pliable. Individual needs have to take a back seat to group considerations. Changing plans for a group of forty is a major enterprise. Changing plans for a group of five is a few quick texts. A smaller youth group is flexible enough (and hungry enough) to be attentive to the students in the group. With fewer students to consider, that smaller youth group can be more intentional about meeting individual needs—even a little outside-the-box intentional. The flexibility of smallness means it's possible to text your whole youth group one evening and organize an instant beach party, picnic, bike trip, work project, and so forth. That freedom for innovation and flexibility can help us be more kid-sensitive. We discover that the power of small transforms questions like "What have we got to lose?" into more of a doorway instead of a dead end.

You'll see that truth in vivid color in this book. I love its focus on real-life stories and real-life youth workers who dare to believe that a big God can do amazing work in a smaller youth group. Listen to them carefully as you read through these pages. You'll hear their names, recognize some of their challenges, and be inspired by their journeys. Hopefully, as you read, you'll also begin to realize their story could be your story.

## THINK BIG WITH YOUR SMALL-ER YOUTH GROUP

So, get ready to have your ministry stretched by what you discover in this book. You'll be invited to imagine the power of small multiplied by the power of God. You'll be challenged to come to terms with the fact that the big question for your youth ministry is not about how many thousands are hungry and needy, but about what you and your church will do with the few loaves and fish you have on hand. You'll be reminded that Jesus pointed to the mustard seed and not the watermelon when he talked about the power of faith (Mark 4:31). And, in the end, I think you'll be compelled to dream about, and practically build toward, a youth ministry limited not by a smaller church, but only by a smaller vision and smaller faith.

Oh, and, by the way, thanks so much for serving Jesus by loving teenagers. Whether it feels like it or not, that's no small thing!

Dr. Duffy Robbins
Professor of Youth Ministry, Eastern University
St. Davids, Pennsylvania
Twitter: @duffyrobbins

# ACKNOWLEDGMENTS

This book is a result of a multitude of people who have mentored me both in life and ministry. I have been blessed to have the opportunity to learn from, partner with, and create lasting relationships with some of the leading youth ministry minds in the world. Each of them inspires me to seek creative and innovative models to equip and empower youth ministry leaders who build ministries that have a lasting impact on faith development of young people.

The creation of the Smaller Church Youth Ministry Initiative was not an instantaneous event. It was built on a foundation that was already laid by those who had created and designed training for youth workers in the Tennessee Conference of The United Methodist Church. That training model, known as Youth Ministry Institute, was instrumental in my development as a youth minister. I am forever grateful for the work and guidance of Rev. Terry Carty and Beth Morris, who trained me as well as hundreds of other youth workers throughout Tennessee. I am grateful for the partnership and commitment of the Martin Methodist College faculty and staff as they help equip and empower ministry leaders. Through Martin Methodist College, I have had the opportunity to partner with Dr. Dominic Nigrelli, Dr. Jack Radcliffe, and Dr. Ed Trimmer. Each of them is instrumental in training youth ministry leaders as well as encouraging me to continue to seek new models of training church leaders to be in ministry with young people.

I must thank my dear friend, cheerleader, colleague, and co-conspirator, Stephanie Caro. From the moment we met in Louisville at the Simply Youth Ministry Conference, Stephanie has been an inspiration for me and the many ministry leaders across the Tennessee Conference. We've spent many hours dreaming and scheming how best to train and develop Smaller Church Youth Ministries not only in Tennessee but throughout the United States. This book could not have been written without her partnership with SCYMI and her cheering me forward in the writing process.

I have an amazing group of folks I get to work with every day at the Tennessee Conference Connectional Ministry office. Jullie Meyer not only keeps me organized, pays the bills, sends out e-mails, and keeps me sane, she also serves on the Smaller Church Youth Ministry Initiative Coaching Team. Jullie is a veteran youth worker who leads with compassion. Todd Cox, who wrote the discussion questions for each chapter, has been a part of our team since I first met him when he was just a seventh-grader. Todd is already an inspirational leader with an amazing future in ministry. Thank you, Bishop McAlilly, Amy, Angela, Izzie, John, Mary Lou, Mary T, Patty, Rita, and Merrilee for the continual encouragement and support. Thank you, Lloyd and Bettye, for believing in me and trusting me with such an important ministry. I would be remiss if I didn't give thanks for the Congregational Development Team of the Tennessee Conference. This team has generously given the funding necessary to provide this vital opportunity to smaller congregations.

I am excited about the present and future impact that the Smaller Church Youth Ministry Initiative is having and will have because of the team of coaches investing in churches. Jullie Meyer, Christine Penner, and Chandra Inglis each is uniquely gifted and passionately called to help churches build sustainable ministry with young people. I am so grateful for the work they do every day to support the churches of the Tennessee Conference. Jullie, Christine, and

Chandra have contributed to the discoveries behind the content of this book.

To the churches and ministry leaders who have trusted us through your participation in the Smaller Church Youth Ministry Initiative, I am forever grateful. Many of you contributed to the content of this book through personal stories, dedication, and prayer. God is doing amazing ministry in and through you. Thank you for the commitment and passion you possess for creating disciples of Jesus Christ for the transformation of the world.

Thank you to my friend and editor, Dr. Jack Radcliffe, for believing in me and the work we have done through the Smaller Church Youth Ministry Initiative. Writing a book was never on my bucket list, but I thank you for pushing me anyway. You have responded to my continual passive-aggressiveness, disjointed paragraphs, and dangling participles with encouragement and confidence. Thank you for sticking with me and pushing me forward.

To Keri and Stephanie, thank you for listening to my whining, reading chapters, giving good and honest feedback, sharing coffee and conversation on Fridays. You both are such a blessing to me, my faith life, and the ministry with young people in the Tennessee Conference.

To my friend Rev. Chip Hunter, I am forever grateful for the opportunity to serve in ministry with you at Epworth United Methodist Church. You are a mentor and a friend, and most importantly you have continued to nurture and deepen my call to ministry.

And most importantly I thank God for my family, Shelley, Maré, and Collins. Thank you for loving me and reminding me that my calling is not only in ministry but first and foremost as a husband and father. Thank you for the ways you remind me of who I am and whose I am. You inspire me daily.

Brad Fiscus
Nashville, Tennessee
September 2016

# CHAPTER 1

# THE POWER OF SMALL(ER)

Where I grew up everything was small: the town, the schools, and the church two blocks from my house. It is a beautiful church and it was my church. Memories of how that congregation helped shape me are as vivid as if they were yesterday. They begin with the married couple who served together as our pastors and move to my service as an acolyte for the first time, with the fear of setting the church on fire. Remembering the smells of the sanctuary, the classrooms, and the basement where we had snacks and talked about Jesus makes me smile. There are the Sunday school teachers, vacation Bible school crafts, and the haunted barn that we would create as a youth group during the Halloween season at a church member's farm. We didn't know our church was small. It was simply our church and we loved it. What we know today about faith formation and discipleship is true: These are the kinds of experiences that make faith stick.

While that church has remained small, many people continue to form relationships with one another and Jesus in that place today. There are people of all ages, young and old, who will spend or have spent sixteen to eighteen years of their lives growing up together. I witnessed this on a recent visit home to pay respects to a family friend who had died. Not only did being there remind me of how this congregation was so vital to my faith journey, but it also assured me that their commitment to nurturing the faith of families like mine remains strong today.

With a college degree in education in hand and a vision of teaching awards, coaching high school wrestling championship teams, and a steady stream of successful students, my wife and I went on to have thirteen years of living our dream. God, though, introduced us to a new vision through two key life events: walking with a friend through the pain of losing his wife to cancer and experiencing our first pregnancy. As we prayed and processed all that was taking place, we felt it would be best if I became a stay-at-home dad. Around the time of that decision, we began attending the small Epworth United Methodist Church in Franklin, Tennessee. It was here we chose to raise our two children. We had no way of anticipating what would happen next.

In 2005, during the dedication service for the new sanctuary that the church had built to accommodate odd-defying growth, Bishop Robert Spain, a retired United Methodist bishop, encouraged the audience not to sit back but to become actively involved in the ministry of Jesus Christ in the world. Later in a meeting at the church parsonage, our pastor shared that the church had plans to hire a part-time youth minister. That fall, I was asked to join the ministry team as the youth minister. Inexperienced and untrained, I said YES! I enjoyed serving at my church but at the same time felt that God wanted me to do more. Over the years, "more" came to involve training opportunities, volunteering for the Tennessee Conference of The United Methodist Church on various teams, and serving in my current role as the conference resource person for children, youth, and young adult ministries. God uses small churches in powerful ways.

## WHY SMALL MEMBERSHIP CHURCHES MATTER

In the Tennessee Conference, approximately 82 percent of the congregations have a worship attendance of 99 or less. Across the United States, researchers have determined that 59 percent of churches have a worship attendance of 7–99 people.[1] The study further revealed that 35 percent of churches in the U.S. have 100–499 worshippers; 4 percent of churches see 500–999 in worship; 2 percent have 1,000–1,999 present; churches with 2,000–9,999 in attendance make up 0.4 percent; and the final .01 percent, or 40 congregations in the U.S., have 10,000 or more in worship.[2]

With our society's obsession on the "bigger is better" mantra, small congregations get lost in the mix. We don't hear the stories of the amazing ways that small congregations are living as Jesus Christ incarnate in the world. Mostly we talk about how the church is dying and overtly blame small churches themselves for their plight. The truth is, there is a different reality we don't see. The Tennessee Conference Smaller Church Youth Ministry Initiative was created because we believe in the power and promise of God's intended reality for small churches.

Yes, congregations are dying and closing each year. But I believe that this death is more about the need for new life than the need to assign blame. Blame doesn't change the outcomes; only a new future can do that. The call we have for churches in the Smaller Church Youth Ministry Initiative is to help them see a new possibility for their future, a future filled with hope that reveals their value in the work of Christ in their communities and neighborhoods.

Imagine having a jar, several rocks of varying sizes, and a bag of sand. The challenge is to get everything into the jar without any of it left over. What would be your plan to make this happen? Would you put the rocks in first or the sand? If I told you that 18 percent of the jar was to be filled by the rocks and 82 percent of the jar with the sand, would that change your plan? In order for the jar to be filled by the sand and the rocks, we would start by putting the rocks in first and then pour in the sand. As the sand flows over the rocks, we will see that it fills the gaps between the rocks, ensuring that the entire jar is filled to the top. But please don't misunderstand the analogy here. This isn't a lesson on priorities. Rocks have their purpose and sand has its purpose. The grain of sand is as important to the task of filling the jar as the rock. In the same way, each size of church has a specific place in the kingdom of God.

There is an old and ongoing debate in the Western church on whether evaluating ministry success by tracking the number of persons present is an effective practice. While numbers satisfy our need to quantify ministry, counting heads has arguably served as a distraction from the mission of Jesus Christ. This measurable, at its core, breeds consumerism, comparison, confusion, and despair and cripples the church in its efforts to achieve the goal presented in the Lord's Prayer—may "your kingdom come, . . . on earth as it is in heaven" (Matthew 6:10, NIV). I believe when we lay this battle to rest, we will begin to see the value of churches of *all* sizes present in the global Church today. A disclaimer: This book is not a defense for the existence of small churches. Rather, I hope to make it clear that size doesn't matter. Effectiveness does.

In the Tennessee Conference, we have come to believe that the way we are to serve churches in obedience to Jesus' command to "go and make disciples" is to seek ways to equip churches and leaders of all sizes for the task. *The Book of Discipline of The United Methodist Church* proclaims that local congregations provide "the most significant arena through which disciple-making occurs."[3] Therefore, we must see the value in the small and the big. Our focus for the churches in the Smaller Church Youth Ministry Initiative is to push back on the societal value to be better than the church next door and instead focus on becoming the community of faith God has created and called each to be. This challenge encourages the discovery of uniqueness and also the need for connection to other faith communities in the community so that every person knows the extent of Christ's love and redemptive power.

## A NEW MODEL

Starting out in my role as the director for young people's ministries for the Tennessee Conference of The United Methodist Church, it was important to listen—a lot. It was clear from listening to youth workers that how we helped churches in ministry with young people needed to change. We had done a good job of training volunteer youth workers designated by the church as the point people to do youth ministry, yet they weren't able to recruit and lead other volunteers. While dreaming about what this new model would be, I met Stephanie Caro, lead consultant specializing in smaller churches, with Ministry Architects. As Stephanie and I began discussing what this new thing would be, I shared about the need of training for small congregations who desired to be in ministry with young people but didn't know where to start. I shared about the passion our small congregations have for discipleship and their struggle at the same time to turn that passion into action. Through my role at the Tennessee Conference, I partnered with Ministry Architects to launch the Smaller Church Youth Ministry Initiative. This initiative is rooted in the deep love that all of us— youth workers, Stephanie Caro, and I—have for the small church.

Over the past five years we have intentionally focused on helping smaller membership churches build teams with systems, structures, and vision around forming ministry with young people that is relationally cohesive and foundationally sustainable. We believe that by building these components correctly, the church will increase its capacity to build disciples. Through the Smaller Church Youth Ministry Initiative, many churches moved from a feeling of limitation fueled by a belief they didn't have enough to a feeling of hope fueled through the lens of a unique calling and a realization that God has already provided everything they need. Transformation takes time, and each church changes differently and with different results. While some have progressed more slowly, others have seen powerful change as they implemented the principles learned through the Smaller Church Youth Ministry Initiative.

## MAKING CHANGE HAPPEN

One of the first challenges that churches in the Smaller Church Youth Ministry Initiative had to overcome is the notion that small churches are abnormal. The 2010 Religious Congregations Membership Study found that the median church in the United States has seventy-five regular participants.[4] The average worship attendance of a United Methodist Church in the United States is eighty-seven persons.[5] In our training cohorts, we discovered church after church limited by its belief in what we call the Small Church versus Small(er) Church Mentality. Phrases such as "We're a small church, so we can't..." and "We're a small church so we don't..." were spoken as kind of a statement of faith. The often used statement "We don't have enough..." was usually completed with *youth, volunteers, money, space, parent involvement,* and so forth. The list, as daunting as it may seem, can be overcome by a change in perspective, processes, and vision. While attendance and participation do affect how ministry can be done, they don't change the call to make disciples.

Churches stuck in a Small Church Mentality are most concerned with saving their church and are often unable to see the opportunity their situation presents to breathe new life into it. Programs are often promoted as the magic bullet. In these cases, young people are often viewed in one of two ways: machinery or scenery.

Alicja Iwanska, a Polish anthropologist, points out that we tend to divide our world into three categories: scenery, machinery, and people. Iwanska found, however, that not all human beings are seen as "people." Iwanska defines *machinery* as "tools people use in their lives to get their work done."[6] Church people are guilty of viewing young people as machinery when they believe that adding youth ministry programs will perform the task of saving their congregations from death.

Churches can also be guilty of viewing young people as scenery, which Ivanska says is enjoyed "in a disinterested sort of way."[7] This perspective values people as decorations or objects to be displayed. Well-intended church leaders demonstrate Iwanska's theory when there is an expectation that young people be seen (being present on Sundays, performing token roles such as holiday programs, or doing manual labor that someone in the church thinks would be a good job for teens) but are not given a voice or place in the life and ministry of the church. Young people, just like their adult counterparts, have much to offer the world in both worship and service.

There are other ways in which smaller churches have become stuck. As the number of smaller churches increases, their health may be worsening. They often appear resilient, weathering the storms of cultural changes, population movements, and denominational neglect and/or efforts to close them, but the onslaught of these challenges takes its toll.

Often inexperienced pastors in their first jobs will envision a new reality for their church. It isn't long before these challenges, limited finances, and the unending mountain of resources and seminars promising solutions overwhelm them and they leave. The church rallies to make it until the next pastor arrives. However, weathering the storm only leaves churches to assess the damage: families who have left, a long list of former pastors, and little hope for a future. The way out of this stuck way of thinking requires a change in perspective, processes, and vision.

William T. McConnell, in his book on congregational renewal subtitled *Healing the Sick, Raising the Dead,* says, "To get to where you want to go, you must first know where you are."[8] Transformation in the smaller membership church is greatly impacted by leaders seeing the current reality and the potential for what can be and inspiring confidence that a new future is possible. This foundational principle motivated us to create a new model with contextually oriented training and coaching based on the hunch that smaller churches could begin to step into their new futures.

Churches in the Smaller Church Youth Ministry Initiative are able to learn and utilize a new framework that helps them shift from the Small Church Mentality to the Smaller Church Mentality. With this new mentality, churches celebrate their size instead of being limited by it. Smaller Church Mentality churches dream God-sized dreams, they are ready for new possibilities, they easily adapt to changes and challenges, and they realize the advantages of being smaller. A smaller church living in the Smaller Church Mentality sees young people for who they are instead of as the machinery to save their church or scenery to make it look hip. Rather, they are viewed as persons with the ability to change the world through their relationship with Jesus Christ. Churches who think Smaller rather than Small understand that numbers matter not because they are comparing themselves to those with more but because each number is a real person who needs to know God's love. The smaller church way of thinking fosters the call for the church to build relationships with the people God has blessed them with so that they can send them out to bless the world.

## ONE CHURCH'S STORY

One of the churches who recognized the need to change their framework from a Small Church Mentality to a Smaller Church Mentality was the Santa Fe Charge in South Central Tennessee. Comprised of four churches, the Santa Fe Charge was a part of the first cohort of smaller churches in 2013. They are served by Rev. Joe Bowers, who has a unique calling to serve multiple smaller church charges. Joe was asked to share his perspective on the effect that the Smaller Church Youth Ministry Initiative had on his ministry with the Santa Fe Charge.

> Living with a clear calling from God to serve the smaller membership church, I responded with joy when contacted concerning a new effort to assist smaller membership churches in our conference with a practical way to address one of our problems, that of having a viable and sustainable

youth ministry. The "Smaller Church Youth Ministry Initiative—2013 Cohort" lasted a year and involved four one-day seminars requiring outside reading assignments, application of the material taught, and coaching calls with Stephanie Caro and my team from the Santa Fe Charge.

The background to this story started several months before when the Santa Fe Charge administrative committee had committed to hiring a part-time youth minister (a full-time student) from Martin Methodist College, located within driving distance of the charge. The charge leadership had responded to my proposal to recruit a student youth minister with mixed response and some hesitation. Two of the churches expressed concern at the value of the effort to their church because they had no youth who attended, while all raised the issue of cost and how to share the expense equally. However, all four churches agreed to humor their pastor with his strange plan and participate in the cohort for the full year. We formed a team with one representative from each church on the charge to participate in the training. By the time the cohort sessions had started, we had hired a young person who was living at home and working part time at a sandwich shop, while attending college at Martin Methodist and working with our charge's youth ministry on alternate weekends.

In one of the chapters of the textbook and during the first training day, the model of what it cost to build a sustainable youth ministry in the local church was presented as a ratio of $1,000 to $1,500 per youth per year. Our charge had committed to investing about $3,000 for our total program for the year. Realizing that we were setting ourselves up for failure or at the very least limited success, I asked our youth pastor how much he was making per week from his job at the sandwich shop. He replied, "About $100 per week." I then asked, "So if we could pay you $200 per month extra, would you consider working with our youth each weekend?" His reply (indicating his disdain for the sandwich shop job) was, "I would change for even less." So I reworked the proposed budget and presented the new idea to the churches. Over the objection and non-commitment of two of the churches, we went ahead with expanding the youth ministry to meet weekly, and thankfully it worked.

Because of our successful increase in the number of youth participating and the overall success of the program, the next year all four churches voted to support our youth minister and our ministry with the youth in the community. We have not achieved the $1,000 to $1,500 per youth per year as recommended by the textbook, but we have approached that number.

The byproduct of this effort in our youth ministry has led to several other cooperative ventures by our four churches. We've also seen invaluable cooperation from other churches in the community, and we now are ministering to the community of Santa Fe with a backpack ministry for children in the local school that provides food for the weekend, an enhanced food pantry ministry housed in one of our churches, and a community-wide 5K run event each year, which raises money for the ministries as well as awareness in the community of our ongoing mission work.

Since Santa Fe's time in the cohort, the youth minister has graduated from college and is now serving a different church while attending seminary. The youth ministry continues to thrive. Because of the efforts of the team developed during the cohort and the faithful work of the youth minister, a strong unit emerged that sustained their ministry with youth while they sought a new college student to serve as their youth minister. Now with a new youth minister on board, the team continues to serve alongside her as partners in ministry. Santa Fe's willingness to adopt a new mental framework was the key to where it is today. This faith community is committed to the ongoing work of building sustainable youth ministry that continues to match this community's God-sized dreams.

This is just one of the stories of churches who participated in the cohort. Transformation does not take place without effort and commitment. Throughout the rest of this book you will have the opportunity to read more from churches who adopted this new framework for ministry in their unique contexts. The concepts discussed in this chapter will also be discussed through their stories.

# STEPHANIE'S RESPONSE

Brad, I love what you're saying here with the whole "small church" versus "smaller church" phraseology. What a great lens to give us as a guide for our outlook! Brad's research numbers are spot on with my research as well. In my training workshops, my experience is that when smaller churches find out the average size church is 75 people, it re-orients them to the fact that THEY are the normal and not the larger "cool church down the street" they think everyone prefers. Some churches use their size as an excuse for not doing great ministry, providing less-than-stellar systems. Imagine the powerful growth toward God that would occur if smaller churches fully understood just how precious is the ministry they bring to the Body's Table!

Since Brad shared his story, I'd better tell mine. How did my love for equipping smaller churches begin? It was accidental . . . or was it? God uses our circumstances, whether created by us or him, to move us where we'll thrive best. It's what God did for me.

I'd been serving in church ministry since the '80s, and the majority of that was spent working in medium/large ministries. All that changed when I got hired on at St. James UMC in St. Petersburg, Florida. I came on staff in 2003 to find eight or nine youths connected to the church. I was clueless about what to do with that; my previous two churches were well over one hundred youths. Who teaches about this stuff? Who could show me how to make the appropriate algebraic adjustments?

I looked around for resources, couldn't find any, and long story short? The folks from Group Publishing/Simply Youth Ministry said, "We don't have many resources to support smaller congregations, so why don't you write/blog/teach it for us?" And so

I did. Despite my large personality, I discovered my wiring is more suited for intimate-number settings in church youth ministry. With smaller numbers than my previous big youth groups, as each youth ministry experience, such as lock-ins and mission project days, passed my calendar, I researched and wrote about it.

My "aha" observations in youth ministry were:

1. Smaller youth groups are easier to manage. Duh!

2. It's easier to make course corrections with a group of ten than a group of one hundred. Spontaneity is nearly impossible with lots of people to contact. Ten kids? One easy phone/mail chain clues everyone in.

3. I knew every kid's name, their siblings' names, their pets' names, and so forth. In other words, less of them meant more of me and the other adults.

4. With fewer kids, we could spotlight each one more. We could get to each Christmas concert and final basketball game.

Friends (old and new through this book), I am so excited to take this journey with you as your church moves to a stronger, thriving ministry to the teenage circles your church intersects. It has been an uber pleasure watching churches grow through the small church cohort-type programs. I've helped lead about a dozen training cohorts now around the country (with five more beginning fall of 2016), and I can tell you this: Small churches who trust the process and the Spirit? They see change. Oh, not an overnight quick fix but through steady tweaking and personalizing their systems. From the ministry principles we study together in each cohort, I've seen God moving as they "square the corners" of their youth ministry. Funny thing is, what happens is that not only does their youth ministry strengthen, but so do the other systems and ministries within each congregation. Amazing, isn't it?

# DISCUSSION QUESTIONS FOR CHAPTER 1: THE POWER OF SMALL(ER)

1. William T. McConnell is quoted in the chapter: "To get to where you want to go, you must first know where you are." Where is your congregation right now? What is the story of your congregation so far?

2. *Visioning* is a word to describe the process of looking toward the future, and praying for what God will do in and through your church next. What is a vision you have of God's leading for your church's Smaller Church Youth Ministry?

# CHAPTER 2

# WHAT IF....?

## PASTOR-CENTERED CHALLENGE

Being the pastor of any size church is a difficult task. In the smaller church, pastors are expected to provide more than great messages. In most places they are the only staff person. These well-intentioned servants have to manage how best to utilize their time so that the mission of their church in the community is being fulfilled and the administrative needs of the entire church are met. In most places, these tasks by themselves can become overwhelming. This is not an indictment of pastors; there are many that provide extraordinary effort to make everything happen.

In the smaller membership church, the challenge to form teams for ministry is daunting for two reasons. One, because they believe they are called to reach all of the people in their congregation and community with the gospel, pastors often find themselves leading all of their church's ministries instead of devoting time to recruit people to help lead those ministries. Second, oftentimes the church expects the pastor to be the central leader of all ministry activity and therefore expects a pastor-centered model. The result of both of these approaches is the same: it is next to impossible to identify and recruit gifted, capable, and willing volunteers.

As pastors and youth ministry leaders across the Tennessee Conference of The United Methodist Church told stories about their struggles to build ministry teams that aligned with the vision of their church, two key areas of learning emerged:

1. The churches who were to participate in the first cohort should display the following characteristics: they were already engaged in youth ministry; they desired a new approach; their pastor was highly supportive; they demonstrated a desire for training and coaching; and they placed a high value on the importance of being connectional and collaborative in ministry with other congregations.

2. It is imperative that the church pastor is involved in the training and coaching program.

To address the challenge of asking for volunteers to form a youth ministry team, each church was required to bring key stakeholders to participate in the training. Key stakeholders are defined as lay leaders, parents, Sunday school teachers, administrative board members, or other influential members of the congregation. We asked each church to send a team of three to five people consisting of the pastor, youth ministry leader(s), and key stakeholders to attend each of the training sessions, engage in the reading assignments and homework, and participate in the coaching calls.

Inviting churches into this new opportunity for training and coaching was challenging. Helping them see that change was both necessary and possible took a lot of persuading. Some of the same pastors and youth ministry leaders who asked for a new model were the same ones who were reluctant to commit their churches to the training and coaching process. Their apprehension was initially due to the way the program was presented. The perception was that we believed their churches were sick or broken. After rephrasing the way churches were asked and better defining the vision for the Smaller Church Youth Ministry Initiative, churches were more than willing to join. The success of churches who previously participated has made recruiting new churches in future cohorts easier.

# ADDRESSING THE "WHAT IFS...?"

When a church is stuck in the Small Church Mentality, it's hard for members to see beyond their church's history and current circumstances. Casting a vision for a new future requires dealing with the fear that keeps them from seeing the opportunity. Moving a church toward the Smaller Church Mentality involves dealing with the what ifs. There's a lot of power in the phrase "What if?" This phrase causes one to examine both sides of the potential outcome of the question.

What follows is a breakdown of some of the what ifs that churches in the Smaller Church Youth Ministry Initiative have examined as they moved toward their new future.

## "What if I just do it by myself?"

This is often the default answer in ministry because it fuels the belief that "I can get it done better and more efficiently." It might seem more expedient to do it by yourself, but it's not the approach we find in Scripture. Throughout the New Testament, Jesus talked about the need for community. He spent a great deal of his time building a team who would become disciples. These disciples continued to share the gospel long after Jesus had ascended to heaven.

Not only is doing ministry alone unbiblical, but it can also limit the depth and reach of the ministry. Research on faith development reveals that as a person develops in his or her spiritual journey, he or she needs many mentors. Multiple mentors help shape a person's faith. Mentors help provide support in times of joy, in times of grief, through the challenges of life, and most importantly in times of doubt.

Paul Tillich, a German-American theologian, said: "Doubt is not the opposite of faith; it is an element of faith."[1] So it is essential then that young people have a variety of mentors who have the ability to help translate life and faith in the midst of their doubt. Dr. Andrew Zirschky of the Center for Youth Ministry Training says this about the importance of mentors and doubt: "If we are going to respond adequately to the doubting experiences of youth, we need to ensure that young people . . . have patient, understanding companions who can guide and care for them through the twists and turns of the journey of doubt."[2] Going it alone limits the ability of a church's ministry with young people to effectively meet the needs of the diverse group of young people with whom the church has been entrusted.

## "What if we don't have volunteers?"

In the smaller membership church, the "go it alone" model is often the default due to the inherent belief that there are not enough volunteers. The good news is that this perspective can be changed by introducing a new understanding of what a youth leader is. The misconception that adults doing ministry with young people have to be young, cool, and childless is ill informed. The reality is that youth leaders come in all ages and stages. Some of the most effective youth leaders often don't even realize their ability to work with teens. The smaller membership church must throw out these old stereotypes surrounding youth leaders and call people who demonstrate a genuine love for young people regardless of age or stage of life. The youth ministry leaders who participated in the Smaller Church Youth Ministry Initiative represent a variety of ages and stages of life and have a unique cool factor that emanates from one place: their love of Jesus Christ. Through training and coaching, they learn that their relevance as youth ministers has little to do with looks and all to do with authenticity of relationships.

Epiphany, a young adult who grew up at Gordon Memorial United Methodist Church in Nashville, was asked to give insight into the impact this intergenerational community has had on her life. Throughout her life and especially now as a college student, her faith community is an ongoing and shaping force in her spiritual life.

> Growing up in church has always had a big influence on my life. A relationship with God is something my parents wanted my sisters and me to pay close attention to. Not only did my

immediate family have a huge impact, but my church family did also. The older members have watched me grow and sprout into the person I'm becoming today. Their influence helped me stay positive that my relationship with God was the most important one. They've always told me that they see something in me that they don't usually see in young people my age. At the time I never really understood what they meant, but as I've gotten older and grown, I realize what they mean. I'm a person whose faith has been tested many times. Sometimes I often question, "God, why me?," but they never let my shakiness steer me away. They said the best thing to do is continue to talk to God and let him know that I am here and present for whatever he has in store for me at the moment. The older members at my church home are the people I look up to. They've always helped keep me on the path I am on today. If it wasn't for them, I would probably be another lost young person searching for guidance.

## "What if we stay the same?"

Mark Oestreicher, a cofounder of The Youth Cartel and lead trainer/coach for its Youth Ministry Coaching Program, says: "As much as some might desire it, or some more cynical might suggest, no church stays the same. They are each in the midst of growing or dying. One key factor in the difference between growing and dying is their posture toward change." An unwillingness to change leads to stagnation. Stagnation leads to decline. Decline leads to death.

God calls us to grow by making disciples who in turn seek out the last, the least, and the lost. This can't be done by staying the same. It requires change in thinking and change in the way ministry happens. Staying the same is safe. Change requires risk.

It was during the Youth Ministry Coaching Program that I learned of the Adizes Principle: all organizations can be seen as living systems. Living systems typically fall into one of two categories: healthy and unhealthy. Only one grows to benefit the world around it. A church is a living system that regardless of size, when healthy, seeks new ways to grow and reach its neighborhood with the good news of Jesus Christ.

Healthy churches dream God-sized dreams and position themselves to reach those dreams. They use their history as a springboard for future ministry rather than as a relic viewed as more glorious than what the present and future will be. Unhealthy churches often become disconnected from their neighborhoods out of a desire for stability and sameness. When a church stops dreaming and creating opportunities to connect with its community, it becomes unhealthy and decline begins to occur. Healthy smaller churches are those who find ways to share Jesus Christ with their community using their unique giftedness.

### Ebenezer Hispanic Fellowship, Nashville, Tennessee

One of the churches who participated in the Smaller Church Youth Ministry Initiative was Ebenezer Hispanic Fellowship, which shared space with 61st Avenue United Methodist Church in Nashville. Ebenezer was just beginning its ministry when it joined the cohort. The leadership had a unique vision and calling to serve a transitional community. As a result, these leaders realized they would build their youth ministry differently than the other churches in the cohort.

While studying their neighborhood, they discovered a large population of young people who played soccer on fields near the church facility. A team of adults committed to faithfully "hang out" on the soccer field to get to know and build trust with this group of teens. The church met their need for refreshment by providing snacks. Oh, and they also began to share the stories of Jesus. Eventually, these young people began to worship with the church and attend youth gatherings. More importantly, Ebebezer Hispanic Fellowship has become "family of faith" for a number of teens they met on the soccer field. What is more, many parents have begun to attend worship with their teens.

Myriam Cortes, the pastor of Ebenezer Hispanic Fellowship, shares this story:

> A young man we met in the community had never heard anything about The United Methodist Church until we started the Soccer Ministry. We supported him even while his family didn't come to church. He has now been involved with us for four years. He had lost hope of going to college since both of his parents are undocumented. He thought college was not for him, and so he started working after high school. Our youth leader encouraged him to apply to college and let God's grace open doors. Before long he got a call from Martin Methodist College to attend school and play soccer there.

> The light in this young man's eyes came to life. Hope came, and as a result his family now sees how the church's love for their child has opened doors for his future. God is at work. God is giving us opportunities to offer Christ to a hurting world.

Ebenezer Hispanic Fellowship is growing because it chose to be healthy.

### "What if we don't have a budget?"

While there might not be a line item in the church's financial statement for youth ministry, money is always available to be spent on young people. The absence of a budget line item means that a clear vision for how and why the money is spent hasn't been created yet.

If this is your story, here are some very simple steps to help give your church leadership a true vision of the financial need:

1. Create a budget that projects the cost of each experience on your calendar. Be sure to think in terms of cost per person. Include the total number involved, both youth and adults. This column will be called "PROPOSED."
2. Keep a good record of where the money you are spending is coming from. Create a column called "INCOME."
    2a. If this money comes from your pocket, STOP!

As long as you are funding the ministry, the congregation won't.

2b. If this money comes from fundraisers, keep a detailed list of who is giving you money. Create a form to be used at checkout for participants to give their contact info. Be sure to indicate how much money people in the congregation are giving through fundraisers or special appeals.

2c. Don't forget to apply for grant-funding opportunities. For example, The United Methodist Church offers grants through the Youth Service Fund.

2d. Send a thank you note to those who donated and give an update on the transformation that occurred from their contribution. ALWAYS send handwritten thank you letters (not e-mail) to donors. Do this within one week of receiving support. Practice this for any fundraiser you do.

3. Create a column where you will subtract the PROPOSED column from the INCOME column to show if you will need to supplement funding (-) or if you have excess funding. Call that column "NEED."

4. Keep a good record of how much you are spending to make ministry happen. If you aren't doing that currently, start today. Plug that information into the budget you prepared in a column titled "ACTUAL."

5. Demonstrate that you are a good steward of the financial resources others have provided by keeping clear records with receipts of expenses. Show this in the "FINAL" column by subtracting the ACTUAL from the INCOME.

6. Share this budget with your pastor, your administrative board, and the finance team.

7. Tell stories of transformation that result from opportunities funded by financial support with your congregation.

An example of a budget:

| Experience | Proposed | Income | Need | Actual | Final |
|---|---|---|---|---|---|
| Mission Trip | $3,000 | $2,800 | ($200) | $2,900 | ($100) |
| Fall Retreat | $1,200 | $1,200 | $0.00 | $1,156 | $44 |
| Spring Retreat | $1,240 | $1,440 | $200 | $1,240 | $200 |

## PARTNERSHIP AND COLLABORATION

Even a limited budget should not limit the ministry you are able to provide. It is merely an obstacle looking for an opportunity. During the first year of the Smaller Church Youth Ministry Initiative, churches seized the opportunity to experience the value of working together. An appeal was sent out to the churches in the Tennessee Conference of The United Methodist Church asking them to inventory and share their curriculum. Many churches, especially some of the larger ministries, had multiple copies of great curriculum sitting unused on shelves. These materials were made available through a central sharing library for cohort churches to use.

A second way the first cohort churches were encouraged to work together was through partnerships. Church ministry teams sat with other church teams to discuss the content of the training and share ideas. As an assignment, churches were asked to partner with a neighboring congregation to do ministry together in some manner. This collaborative effort inspired them to create new opportunities to partner with others. In some places youth ministries combined to do retreats. Others held combined worship and teaching events; others planned and participated in mission opportunities. While money is a critical resource for doing ministry, the power of collaboration and connection can overcome this obstacle and have a multiplying effect.

### Hillsboro First UMC, Hillsboro, Tennessee

Hillsboro First United Methodist Church discovered the power of connection and collaboration. The husband-and-wife team of

Kelly and Mandy Smith serves as the youth ministers of this church southeast of Nashville. Having grown up in the Hillsboro church, they were asked to take on the role of youth ministers when their son entered middle school. Mandy reflects on their experience:

> During the cohort, we learned the importance of connection. Not only were we in the training with other churches our size, but we were also asked to partner with a neighboring church to plan an activity together. As a result, our churches have come together several times. Our youth loves the opportunity and connection. That youth minister of the neighboring church and I now have a close relationship. We rely on each other for sharing ideas, resources, and support. Our young people now have built friendships with each other. The impact on our church goes beyond youth ministry. Our whole church from children's ministry through older adults is growing stronger due to becoming more connected to the churches in our area.

## "What if we grow?"

Over the past ten or so years, denominational leaders and pastors have kept a close eye on church growth/decline statistics, headlines, and commentary. At a Catalyst Conference I attended several years ago, I recall Andy Stanley, pastor of North Point Community Church in Atlanta, saying that churches in decline didn't set out to be that way—they ended up there because they forgot to help parishioners find a place to serve in the life of the church. A church living through the Smaller Church Mentality sees each person as having the ability to participate in ministry. A team of called and committed leaders who take hold of the opportunity to learn together, share each other's gifts for ministry, and dream and plan together will grow in confidence and other ways that can't be quantified. Confidence itself is key to a strong foundation for taking risks and evaluating new opportunities to serve a community.

A Japanese proverb says: "Vision without action is a daydream. Action without vision is nightmare." A clear vision and strategy to accomplish it are the first building blocks to a thriving Smaller Church ministry with young people. As your team grows together and serves together to implement the strategy, you will begin to see growth in youth participation in your church.

## Westland UMC, Lebanon, Tennessee

Mandy Rogers is the youth minister at Westland United Methodist Church in Lebanon, Tennessee. Westland joined the Smaller Church Youth Ministry Initiative as Mandy was beginning her second year of ministry.

> My first year in youth ministry was a nightmare. I had very few students, and more than once only one kid showed up at youth group. Talk about awkward. Some students and parents felt betrayed by the previous youth minister's short-lived tenure at the church, and, to others, I would never measure up.
>
> I would lie awake at night worried, stressed, insecure, incapable. I felt like a failure. I found out about the Smaller Church Youth Ministry Initiative toward the end of that first year and applied for the program. Throughout the next year, I was both encouraged and challenged by youth ministry veterans.
>
> The very first requirement of the program was to formulate a team, consisting of four other adults and me, who would travel to cohort training and face-to-face coaching four times during the year. The team included our senior pastor, our lay leader, a volunteer, and a parent. Instantly, I had a team of people who could share my burden and were invested in our ministry. And that was just the beginning.
>
> The program wasn't designed to just be important talking points. During one of our quarterly training days, we actually sat down together to set goals, benchmarks, and important next steps.

Back at home between meetings, our team worked together to implement what we learned in the areas of recruiting volunteers, creating a fifteen-month calendar, spreading the importance of intergenerational relationships, and building a student leadership team.

Two years later, we have tripled the size of our youth group. And we are still working on implementing the strategies we learned. We gained so much information that we couldn't possibly do it all at once—that would have been overwhelming, except for that whole "team" concept. We simply worked on what we could at the time and we continue making adjustments along the way to get where we want to be.

There's no magic formula, but the foundational elements I learned through the cohort gave me not only the knowledge to build our ministry but the confidence to follow through.

Often the obstacle to this type of growth is a lack of clear communication and long-range planning. Churches who develop calendars that provide information with a fifteen- to eighteen-month view are more successful at involving their current over-scheduled congregants as well as attracting new participants from the community. The time that Mandy and her team spent developing their vision and plan for ministry has resulted in the numerical growth they've seen during the past two years. Building a foundation correctly takes time and intentionality. As Mandy and her team continue to grow in confidence for ministry together, they will continue to have the courage to take risks and evaluate new opportunities to engage in ministry in their neighborhood.

Each of the ministry leaders and congregations who gave input into this chapter has explored both sides of the "What if?" questions they've wrestled with. Having the courage to ask, "What if?" is the first step toward a new future. What are the what ifs your church needs to answer?

# STEPHANIE'S RESPONSE

Brad, you've done a great job here laying out the positive effects for churches when they take a leap, a chance, into unclear ministry waters. You've told the tales of several congregations who took risks despite their fears and came out on top. So encouraging!

My reader friends, would you think less of me if I counter-commented with "What if you don't?" I hope not because I'm going to do it anyway. It's not true confession time; you won't have to call a hotline and share "less-than-successful" stories when your ministry played things just a little too safe or held on to "old school" when "new and fresh" would have been the way to go. I'd like to make sure we know what shortsighted thinking looks and sounds like so we know how to navigate around it toward the "what if" possibilities.

Let me tell you a story...

*Once upon a time there was a thriving small church, the kind of church who had to set up extra rows of chairs every major holiday Sunday. "Thriving" looked like a full choir loft, overflowing classrooms, and lots of programming.*

*But the 1990s arrived and church times were changing, which is really nothing new since the only thing that doesn't change is change itself. When change came knocking on the door of this church, the leaders answered and said, "No, thank you. We're obviously doing fine just the way we are. See? We're full." The church stayed the same stalwart it always had been.*

*The 2000s blew in and all around this church? Change was flourishing in the neighborhood. People wanted their communication electronically. Clothing choices for going anywhere, including church, leaned toward an easier lifestyle. The spectrum for musical preferences had broadened from good ol' organ music on one end all the way to guitar, keyboards, and drums on the other. All this change followed new people into churches, but this church? It was confident in sticking to what had worked so well all those years ago.*

*Signs of wear and tear began to show at the church. Not only were no extra chairs set out, but the church also had to begin roping off sections of its seating so that attendance looked fuller and the crowd looked bigger. A guitar and drums were allowed to make an appearance at a time other than the "regular" service as long as any signs of their existence were hidden before the "regular" service began. The church fought over getting "that newfangled" Internet, when forms and pencils and typewriters would still work, right?*

*And let's talk about the clothing police. Without official approval, they had apparently opened up a satellite office at this church. "Tickets" in the form of dirty looks and cruel comments were given out frequently, especially to those wearing hats, shorts, and tattoos in church.*

*You may be wondering how "different" people felt and fit in at this church, whatever "different" means to you. Honestly? They didn't even try. The church's reputation was out there now that "different" wasn't welcome, so "different" didn't even come through the doors of the church.*

*Overarching was the attitude, "We used to be something." Much-needed change was viewed as an unholy thing, and the safety of "Let's do nothing because we'll offend someone" was embraced.*

*The 2010s came and the church knew it was in trouble. Serious trouble. By the mid 2010s, it was too late. There were too few members left, and those members had no emotional energy. Sadly, finally, the church recognized and regretted ignoring the several key "what if" crossroads that had come its way. The church had gone from having a full-time pastor to a very part-time chaplain, which was all it was going to need. That, and someone to turn out the lights as the last person left.*

So here's my list of "What if we don't?" for small churches to move forward:

- Is this decision about a building or is it about someone's eternal salvation?

- In the early church, the organ was considered a pagan instrument and was banned for years. Is a fight over drums or guitars really so tragic?

- Screens are just screens, people. Put them in the sanctuary if they'll help. After all, a microphone system was new at some point, right?

- Listen to your young people about how they'd like to do things.

- Just because it used to work doesn't mean it will work now.

- It's not about the church member who already knows Jesus. It's about the ones who don't.

To me, the best thing you've read in this chapter is the story Brad told of Ebenezer Hispanic Fellowship. Let me fill in a few details in a nutshell: NO youth were coming through their church doors. At most they got two kids to come and they were the pastor's and leader's kids. So Ebenezer church took the gospel of Jesus Christ to the soccer field, passed out snacks, water, and so forth. Know how many youth came to their next youth group (which they held on the field before the games)? Forty-seven. There's a "what if" for you.

# DISCUSSION QUESTIONS FOR CHAPTER 2: WHAT IF...?

1. Identify the key stakeholders within your congregation. How have they engaged with and participated in youth ministry so far, and how could they be challenged to be engaged more?

2. Identify people who are mentors in your congregation. How have they helped you grow as a Christ follower or leader? How can you use what you have learned from them to become a mentor for young people?

3. Identify three diverse people in your congregation you believe God is calling to volunteer as youth leaders. What gifts do they bring that could help young people and the youth ministry thrive? What could this team accomplish together?

4. Identify places in the community where young people gather. How can the congregation reach out to this group in their natural environments? How can what you learn about the places that make them feel comfortable help you create an inviting atmosphere for them in your congregation?

# CHAPTER 3

# BUILDING

## START

You'll never get to where you're going until you take the first step. Take my (Brad's) story, for example. I learned to create stained-glass art when I turned thirty-five. My daughter—our oldest child—was one year old. Now, fifteen years later, hundreds of pieces of art have been created, given away, or sold to people throughout the world. In my spare time I teach others how to create stained glass as a Sabbath practice.

Long ago, I chose to believe that I wasn't an artist. Somewhere along the way, I began to believe that to create art meant I had to know everything about art. To produce perfect pieces of art, I had to be the perfect artist. That belief or "script" kept me from discovering my God-given skills and talent for quite some time. I never imagined that I was a stained-glass artist until I started.

The biggest challenge we face in starting something is our expectation that it all has to be perfect. Perfection is the enemy of good and often the barrier to starting. God doesn't expect us to be perfect, but we are expected to start, to move, to create. Ephesians 2:10 says: "Instead, we are God's accomplishment, created in Christ Jesus to do good things. God planned for these good things to be the way that we live our lives."

So how does my story of discovery as a stained-glass artist relate to youth ministry? Just start. Take the first step. Whether it is the first piece of stained glass or your church's youth ministry, when you listen and respond to the Holy Spirit's voice to simply begin with the gifts, skills, and direction God has given, you can build your church's ministry with young people. It doesn't matter how many youth you have. What does matter is that there are some folks willing to help young people realize how much God loves them.

A caution: If you are looking at starting a youth ministry as a way to save a church in decline, please don't. Young people need the Savior, not the pressure of being a savior.

OK, let's say you have passionate adults and you've got some young people. You're probably wondering where to start. It's been our experience with smaller churches in the training cohort that the first step in starting a ministry with young people is to get the critical stakeholders on board.

The key stakeholders in starting a youth ministry include:

- All potential youth group members (of course);

- Their parents;

- Other adults who are interested (who might just discover they're called to serve on the ministry team); and

- Most importantly, the pastor and several key leaders in the church.

We've found that getting these people in a room together for dialogue is the first step. We call this a visioning meeting. It is a time of asking questions, listening, and taking notes on large sheets of paper. We've found it best to break the group into subgroups of four to six people. Each group will discuss the same questions and then share their input with the larger group. This approach makes room for more persons to share and be heard. As you gather the responses from the questions, look for similarities, look for new insights, look for opportunities to create a unique ministry with young people.

To begin the dialogue about gaining a vision for youth ministry, you might ask questions such as:

- Who are the young people in our congregation and in our community?

- What do the young people in our congregation and community need?

- How can our church meet those needs?

- What assets do this congregation and community possess to assist in ministry with young people?

- What challenges do your congregation and community face as a barrier to ministry with young people?

- What goals do we hope this ministry will achieve?

- Who are the people in our congregation and community who value young people?

It is essential that the young people in the room have the chance to participate fully. You'll discover they have much to offer! You might just be surprised when their reason for starting this ministry is more deeply connected to Jesus Christ than many of the older perspectives in the room. (We'll go deeper into this later.)

What if you've already started? If you are like most of us, you're already living in the house while renovating it, as my friend Mark DeVries likes to say. Whatever analogy seems to fit your situation, the most important thing we can do is bring people together to pause, gain a vision, and plan.

When my wife was pregnant with our first child, we decided to add on to our house. We had to navigate life, pregnancy, and dust. LOTS OF DUST. What a mess! At one point we loaded up the dog, some food, and other necessities and moved into a hotel down the street for a few days while they finished the floors. Don't misunderstand; sometimes that's the way life goes. You have to capture the moment when you have the right resources to begin so that starting does happen. That's why even though we recognized some (not all) of the potential challenges of adding on to our house while pregnant, we did it anyway—and with a plan.

Ministry, especially youth ministry, often operates the same way, and many of the churches in the Smaller Church Youth Ministry Initiative experienced renovating their youth ministry while it happened. They learned that building without a plan might work in the short term but it will leave you with a ministry for the short term. Entrepreneur Abe Reichental projects this thought that can be applied here: "We're not building a future for a few years, we're building for a lifetime."[1] Building for a lifetime requires careful attention to the things that result in sustainability.

Simon Sinek, who wrote the leadership book *Start With Why*, shares that we most often focus on what we do instead of why we do it. He goes on to say that until we pause to consider the *why*, we can never truly understand how to have the greatest impact.[2] We must seek to build with a clear understanding of why we are building. If *what* we are building is not connected to our *why*, we're wasting our time. So while you continue with the youth ministry you have started, pause for a moment, pull a group of youth, parents, and stakeholders together, and ask the questions. Take time to ask, listen, and understand. This will help you formulate a deeper understanding of the *why* for your ministry.

Once you're clear on the *why*, you'll start to see where you want to go. The temptation to avoid is to begin to move in the new direction without a strategy to get there. It is important to take the time for a strategy that flows from a clear understanding of *why* you are in ministry to take shape. Your strategy will include the *who* and the *what* components necessary to achieve the vision. Together, these parts will form the foundation for the ministry—the stability needed to build a sustainable ministry.

## HOW TO BUILD

In his book *Sustainable Youth Ministry: Why Most Youth Ministry Doesn't Last and What Your Church Can Do About It*, Mark DeVries notes that the passion for ministry with young people must be matched with an intentional process for building the systems to guide the ministry.[3] From the start, the Smaller Church Youth Ministry Initiative aligned itself with Mark DeVries' company, Ministry Architects, out of a desire to help churches engaged in the cohort build the systems necessary for long-term ministry. Ministry Architects describes this need as "laying a foundation" while "continuing to do ministry." Using a church as a visual, the organization describes the need to lift the church so that the foundation can be built underneath it.

The first of the foundational components is forming a team (which was discussed in the previous chapter). If we're honest, when we are thinking of whom we want to work with, we tend to choose people who are most like ourselves. While it's important to have like-minded people who truly care about ministry with young people, a strong team should have diversely gifted members. As part of the commitment to joining the Smaller Church Youth Ministry Initiative, churches were given specific identifiers of who should participate in the training and coaching process. Those identifiers ensured that each church would be positioned to recruit the best team possible for effective ministry.

While we believe it is important to shift from the pastor-centered model of ministry, having the pastor on board will help ensure that the youth ministry is integrated into the ministry of the church. To avoid the potential problem of the pastor running the show, the team leader must be someone else. The pastor doesn't have to be involved in the day-to-day functioning of the ministry, but he or she does need to be a part of the foundation-building, which includes the critical function of providing the theological framework that connects the why, who, and what.

Passionate people who are gifted at engaging in relationships with young people will become the team leader(s). The congregation should support these people through prayer, first and foremost, but additionally through opportunities for skill development and spiritual renewal so that their passion and giftedness are both recognized and enhanced.

The remaining members of the team will be the stakeholders. This group of people is essential to help connect the ministry to the rest of the congregation. They serve as a support network and seek out other adults to participate in the church's ministry with young people. Key stakeholders provide an important line of communication between the ministry team and the congregation, especially as it relates to paying the rent.

Paying the rent is essential to the foundation-building process. Ministry Architects describes three rents that a ministry should pay in order to have room for creativity, risk-taking, and innovation. Ministries that fail to pay these rents experience discouragement, distrust, and second-guessing within the broader congregation. The key stakeholders help ensure that the rents are paid but also that the ministry team is informed should the rent expectations change.

The three rents are numbers, programs, and enthusiasm.

## THE RENT OF NUMBERS

While focusing on numbers should not be the main metric of a vibrant youth ministry, numbers do matter. As part of the building process, establishing an agreed expectation for the number of young people actively involved in the ministry is vital. Not doing so will open the door for criticism. Setting this number together from the beginning will help provide clarity as you move forward. As a baseline, Ministry Architects suggests 10 percent of the worshipping congregation as a place to start. Ministry Architects also discovered that many ministries experience difficulty expanding numbers to more than 20 percent of the worshipping congregation.[4] Both of these parameters will help dispel differing perspectives that each stakeholder might have.

## Assessing involvement

Numbers matter because people matter. Start by creating a list of all of the young people who are connected to your congregation. Making the list will help you determine who is engaged and who is not. Set this list up with some categories that indicate the level of involvement for each young person in the church based on points of connection. Points of connection can be defined as Sunday school, worship, youth group, youth events, or other church-related activities.

These categories of involvement may include any or all of the following:

1. **Inactive:** Youth in this category are on the rolls but do not attend any point of connection. This may include youth whose parents attend but the youth does not. This may also include youth whose siblings attend but they do not.

2. **Engaged:** Youth in this category are those who attend at least one or two times during the year.

3. **Involved:** Youth in this category are those who attend any point of connection at least one time a month.

4. **Invested:** Youth in this category are those who attend any point of connection at least one time a week.

You can use this list as a tool to help your team set goals to increase participation with youth connected to your congregation. It will help you formulate a plan to connect with those who are inactive, and it will help you focus on opportunities that will move each young person toward being highly invested in the ministry.

## THE RENT OF PROGRAMS

While attendance is important, we all will agree that ministry is more than teens showing up. What God does in the midst of your youth gatherings is what really matters. Those gatherings, also called programs, are the *what* of ministry and are key to accomplishing the *why* of the ministry. As the second rent, programs that are clearly aligned with the mission and vision for the ministry ensure that this payment is made.

So how do you ensure mission and vision alignment? As you design your ministry and create the programs that will help you reach your vision, include the following:

1. **Parent involvement:** Parents are the greatest influencers of their children's faith. Vibrant ministries seek ways to create opportunity for faith connections between parents and their children.

2. **Acceptance:** A vibrant ministry creates a space where unconditional love is valued and where accountability and support are provided in that love.

3. **Belonging:** A vibrant ministry is one where individuals are celebrated for their uniqueness and giftedness from God.

4. **Cause:** A vibrant ministry will seek a greater purpose into which the community will pour its collective passions, resources, and talents in order to bring God's kingdom to earth as it is in heaven.

5. **Leadership development:** A vibrant ministry that makes room for young people to lead and give input is one that

will have a higher number of invested members. (We will go into leadership development in detail in a later chapter.)

6. **Culture of call:** A vibrant ministry will seek opportunities for those involved to discover and discern how God might be calling them to serve in pastoral ministry.

All of these components are necessary pieces of an effective discipleship process. Being intentional about including them will help create programs that lead youth to build lasting faith that is connected to the church and the world.

## THE RENT OF ENTHUSIASM

When a ministry has spent time developing programs that are well planned, clearly communicated, and engaging, this gives youth and parents something to talk about that helps to generate the third rent: enthusiasm.

Without enthusiasm for the youth ministry and the ministry team, achieving the vision will be difficult. Enthusiasm is the fuel that helps move the ministry forward not only in the good times but also in the more challenging times. When there is joyful enthusiasm, trust is built between the church leadership and the team leading the ministry. When enthusiasm is waning, it may suggest that volunteers are overburdened and/or feel underutilized in the roles they play in the ministry.

As you build your team, pay your rents through planning for ministry. Most importantly, as you build disciples, remember that you are building for a lifetime. The ministry you are building and leading today will have a rippling effect across time as each person lives out the message of the gospel.

**Bethel United Methodist Church, Murfreesboro, Tennessee**
Christi Allen is the volunteer youth ministry leader at Bethel United Methodist Church in Murfreesboro, Tennessee. Christi shares:

I am forever grateful for attending the Smaller Church Youth Ministry Initiative because our church grew as a cohesive unit in its approach to the youth program, certain issues were highlighted as improvement areas in the program, and it allowed me (as a volunteer youth leader) to listen and learn from other small-church youth programs.

As a group, we developed procedures and processes on volunteer requirements. We identified the types of households our youth are being raised in. We also created new ideas on how to make important connections within the church for retention purposes and true Christian living.

The ingeniousness of SCYMI is in bringing the pastor, a youth parent, a member of the congregation, and youth leaders together to discuss and create a vision and mission. By combining all these individuals with one goal of furthering and defining youth ministry within the church, it created a unified responsibility to invest in the youth of the church.

# STEPHANIE'S RESPONSE

Brad, you're on the money with this chapter. In all the church consulting work I do for Ministry Architects, this topic is my Number 1 passion/soapbox, the hill worth dying on, in helping churches get to where they want to go—by helping them simply get going. Period.

It's July as I'm writing this and we're almost on top of the 2016 Summer Olympics in Rio. For the first time ever, a male swimmer from the United States will be competing in his fifth Olympics. Can you believe it? Think of all that it takes to get to even just one Olympics: the practices, the meets, the early mornings, the late nights. And Michael Phelps is just the man who's done it for a fifth one. How he does at the Games will be determined before this book meets printed page. But the point I'm making won't change: Michael Phelps didn't just wake up one day and say, "I'm going to be a Super Olympian." Well, maybe he did, but the thought didn't end there. He turned it into action.

His first step was to decide the direction he was headed in, and then he began to swim that way. At some point and time, and I bet it was early on in the form of a coach, he asked others for help because they had been where he hadn't and they knew how to get there. So with the help of a bunch of people, he laid out a strategy, a plan. This plan included the who, what, why, when, where, and how of his goal of medaling. Once the dreamed-about plan became pen and ink, he took a lap and then another and then another. He didn't waiver, even when he faltered. He just kept swimming and he reached his goal with positive intentionality and directed purpose. It was hard work and it paid off.

My church friends, a Michael Phelps dynamic is what most of our churches are missing. We know we're ready to do something. We know we want an active, growing youth ministry. The missing piece filling the gap? A very intentional plan, the strategy, so to speak, that will get us from Point A to Point C. In other words, Point B, the plan.

I have a pastor friend, Rev. Jeff Clinger, who serves in the Great Plains Conference of The United Methodist Church. I've been spending time with his church consulting in this very area of its leadership and forward movement. Pastor Jeff said to me on one visit, "We know where we want to go. Our problem is we don't have the strategy on how to get there."

A definition for strategy? Hard work. The actual journey of "doing," not the pre-planning of "talking." This is the sticking point for most churches. Lots of churches have great leadership teams who make great decisions . . . , then leave the meeting, nothing having been accomplished. Why? Because they fail to do the work of creating a detailed plan. People at the table think someone else will do it (and that "someone else" is usually the church staff who are already at the too-much-work and not-enough-hours stage).

People at the table need to ask themselves key questions such as:

- How are we going to accomplish this goal?

- How do we explain the rationale behind this plan so others will "get it"?

- Who's going to be on the team to do it?

- What staff will we need?

- What volunteers will we need?

- What's the timeline?

- What approvals are needed?

- What data is needed?

- What calendar space?

In my conversation with Pastor Jeff, he said:

> It's a lot like the *South Park* episode called "Underpants Gnomes." The story line is that the gnomes come in the middle of the night and steal the underwear from the bedrooms of the city's residents. One night, the South Park gang follows the gnomes down into the tunnels to check out what the gnomes were really up to. The main gnome says:
>
> "Phase One: Collect Underpants. Phase Two: . . . "
>
> (And the screen goes black for a moment.)
>
> "Phase Three: Profit."
>
> Stephanie, First United Methodist Church is like the Underpants Gnomes: We have step one and three. What we don't have is step two—the strategy.

(Watch a clean thirty-five-second clip of the episode on YouTube at *tinyurl.com/jmmdq85*.)

Coming up with the game plan strategy isn't that hard. E-mail me at Stephanie@ministryarchitects.com and I'll send you a template, or go to our website at *ministryarchitects.com* and you can download one.

The hard part? The work of getting it done. But the reward? A youth ministry where students feel loved, where church members know their names and celebrate their milestones. A church who will live on past ten years because leaders are being raised up from birth. And the reward of that? Imagine being on the Olympic Medals platform, wearing a medal. Meeting your youth ministry goals feels even better than that. Imagine!

# DISCUSSION QUESTIONS FOR CHAPTER 3: BUILDING

1. Chapter 3 begins by describing the visioning process. What are some of the unique goals, mission points, or issues that will play a factor in shaping your growth (for example, poverty levels, rural versus urban, elevated unemployment rates, and so forth)?

2. The *why* versus *what* debate is a key part of this chapter, and Brad identified the importance of "why" and how "what" will follow. With that, why are you building this ministry? What is influencing this initiative most? What is motivating you?

3. What youth-friendly programs are happening in your church now? What makes them youth-friendly? How open are the other programs to young people? How can these be revitalized to be open and inviting to young people as well as middle- and older-age congregants?

# CHAPTER 4

# LEADING

Now that you are building the foundation, you are on your way to creating a dynamic ministry with young people. Did you notice the end of that sentence? It says: ministry with young people. Ministry with young people is different from ministry to or for young people. When you're engaged in ministry with young people as opposed to ministry to or for young people, you invite them into leadership. Ministry with young people promotes the belief that young people and adults are in partnership together. Ministry to or for young people implies that ministry is something for young people to consume. A ministry with young people empowers them to seek out how God is calling them to be transformed and in turn transform the world for Jesus Christ. So how do you create a ministry with young people type of ministry?

## DEVELOP LEADERS

Leadership development is a key component of a vibrant ministry with young people. When you make room for young people to have a voice and a role, you won't be disappointed. They have much to offer and they want to contribute. I heard one young man put it this way: "Adults in ministry are often willing to let young people set the up the banquet tables, but they seldom give young people a seat at the banquet." Those are some biting words. They want a seat at the table, not just to share in the banquet but to help create and design it so that those they care about will feel welcome to the banquet.

There is risk to making room for others to lead. What if they don't do it the way you do it? What if they make a mistake? Both will happen. The truth is, is it's a far bigger mistake to not take the risk of giving them space to lead. Creating opportunity for students to lead is an essential component of a sustainable youth ministry. Empowering young people with this responsibility even as they wrestle in and with their faith provides opportunity for deeper learning, skill development, and call discernment. In the midst of the synergistic relationship of success and failure, learning takes place. Youth ministries that seek ways of including young people in the process of visioning, planning, and creating see vibrancy that is not experienced in places where ministry is done to or for them.

In the Smaller Church Youth Ministry Initiative we encourage ministry leaders to include young people in leadership of all aspects of the youth ministry. As the objections begin, we simply remind them that historically young people were at the forefront of every significant Christian movement throughout history. Who better than young people know young people? I'm not advocating for churches to seek out youth ministry leaders who are young as a way to reach young people. However, I am advocating that you utilize the people, both adults and youth, you already have. Young people are much wiser than they're given credit for. They create amazing ideas to engage the congregation in worship and in mission and they know how to connect with their peers in ways we never will.

## MENTORING TO LEAD

In the balance of making this space for leadership available, young people need caring adults who will demonstrate leadership while equipping and empowering them to lead. As daunting as it may seem, mentoring-oriented discipleship is rather uncomplicated. We only need to look at how Jesus mentored his disciples.

It is believed that most if not all of the apostles were teenagers when Jesus invited them to follow him.[1] His approach to rabbinical leadership wasn't common among religious leaders in his time. While sharing life with his small band of disciples, he revealed who he was and his mission through his teaching, the miracles he performed, and the relationships he fostered. He gave sight to the blind, healed lepers, rescued outcasts, and raised the dead while teaching listeners about life in the kingdom of God. The band of young followers not only had a front row seat, but they also were invited by Jesus to experience it and participate in it with him. Through the way that Jesus influenced the disciples, the way that he shared ministry with them, and the manner in which he taught humility and accountability, Jesus created a team focused on transforming their world and the world to come. Jesus led small and the impact was *big*.

As a young person, my call and passion to lead were nurtured by caring adults who equipped and empowered me as I awkwardly experimented with my gifts and abilities. Who I am today was formed in those leadership moments. Their model of leadership challenged me to be creative, to share ideas, to solve problems, to make decisions, to be inclusive of all persons, and most of all to serve.

Unfortunately, those important moments of learning and growth came from my experiences in school rather than church. At church, I was given the traditional opportunities of reading Scripture and serving as an acolyte. Adults filled most of the ministry leadership roles. I would have loved to have served my church in the ways my school allowed. The lesson for us is this: the church should and can be the place where leaders are developed. I am convinced that as we provide space for young people to lead in our ministries, we will have a greater impact on our neighborhood as we then send our young leaders out to transform the world.

## CHARACTERISTICS OF LEADERS

I've learned from my years in education that giving young people a place to grow and develop as leaders should be an important focus for a congregation. As I transitioned into vocational ministry, it became a priority of mine to create opportunities for young people to lead. I have been blessed beyond measure by the experience of sharing leadership with young people. What comes next are some key characteristics of leaders that I share with the young people I serve with. As we explore them, ask yourself how you might equip and empower young people in the ministry you serve by developing these characteristics in them.

## Leaders are followers

The most effective leaders understand what it means to be followers. This understanding promotes empathy. Leaders in the church must first be followers of Jesus Christ. This is our central calling. In Matthew 4:19 (NIV), Jesus called out to Peter and Andrew: "Come, follow me, . . . and I will send you out to fish for people." Peter and Andrew immediately dropped their nets and followed him. As they followed, Jesus taught them many things, but along the way, he empowered them to lead.

## Leaders are trustworthy

Trust is the hardest thing to gain and the easiest to lose. Trustworthiness is demonstrated as the leader shows he or she has the best interests of the team in mind. Trust is reciprocal. Leaders must also trust their team members. It's hard to be trusted if trust is not also given. Trustworthiness requires congruency of words and actions. This means leaders must do as they say. Leaders build trust by supporting their team members through the good times and the bad times. They avoid gossip and cynicism while offering praise and appreciation. As the team grows to trust each other and the leader, the team grows stronger.

## Leaders are learners

A key aspect of leadership is seeking new knowledge. Leading from a humble, learning posture allows space for others to share their ideas, their knowledge, and their gifts. This is a paradigm shift for many in leadership. There is a false notion that the leader has to be the expert. Leading while learning gives a young person the opportunity to gain new skills, new relationships, and new opportunities.

## Leaders are listeners

A leader needs to listen more than she or he speaks. This is a vital part of the learning element of leadership. It's important that we help young people learn how to listen. We live in an immediate response culture, but listening requires us to pause and process. There was a popular Facebook meme that shared this statement: "The biggest communication problem is we do not listen to understand. We listen to reply." Leaders must listen fully in order to understand the needs of the community and the team they are leading. One of my mentors, Rev. Dr. Vin Walkup, taught me the seven-second rule for listening, and I share it with my student leaders. The seven-second rule means that after someone finishes speaking, everyone must pause for at least seven seconds before speaking. Dr. Walkup says this gives our brain time to process the words spoken, which will allow a more thoughtful response to be formulated. It works, I use it.

## Leaders are servants

Leaders must be willing to serve others in order to truly lead. Jesus modeled servant leadership. Throughout his ministry with the disciples he modeled how to be "other" focused. In Mark 10:42-45, Jesus explains what it means to be a servant leader: "You know that the ones who are considered the rulers by the Gentiles show off their authority over them and their high-ranking officials order them around. But that's not the way it will be with you. Whoever wants to be great among you will be your servant. Whoever wants to be first among you will be the slave of all, for the Human One didn't come to be served but rather to serve and to give his life to liberate many people." Leaders who lead as servants exhibit that leadership as a lifestyle, not a position.

## Leaders are mission-focused

Being focused on accomplishing the mission of the ministry is a
key element of leadership. As the team works together to achieve
their goals, distractions can spring up, and the leader's role is to
help redirect the team toward the mission. The leader empowers
the team to seek out the resources and skills needed to achieve it.
Howard Thurman, advisor to Martin Luther King, said this about
being mission-focused: "Don't ask what the world needs. Ask what
makes you come alive and go do it, because what the world needs is
people who have come alive."[2] Leaders who are inspired to achieve
the mission inspire others to join in with them.

# I DO, WE DO, YOU DO

As we equip and empower young people to lead, it's important that
we not leave them to fend for themselves. It's also equally important
to help them learn accountability. I utilize the "I do, We do, You do"
model of empowerment. It's also known as the "Gradual Release of
Responsibility" model.[3]

While in the "I do" mode, I am teaching them about their role and
about the goal of the task, and I'm modeling what leading looks
like. As they are learning in the "I do" mode, they are actively
listening by asking clarifying questions and discussing scenarios
that they may face as they assume leadership.

In the "We do" mode, we are actively engaged in the task together.
I spend part of this time modeling how to lead while gradually
giving up responsibility. Here I begin to shift from being the "doer"
to being the "observer" while they shift from "observer" to "doer."
Additionally, I may provide direct assistance in times of struggle.
I'm not a believer of the "let them fail and they'll figure it out" form
of learning. I believe that while discovery is important, providing
information is necessary, especially if it prevents them from
experiencing discouragement.

The third mode of gradually releasing responsibility is "You
do." During this part of the process, the new leader assumes

responsibility for the task. My role shifts to fully observing—watching as they lead, providing support as needed, giving feedback when necessary, and assessing if the new leader understands what he or she is being asked to do. If I sense a lack of understanding, I provide feedback by asking questions. While asking questions of the new leader, I am first listening and then evaluating what new information needs to be shared and what new skills need to be developed or supplemented. Through this process of releasing responsibility, new leaders build the confidence necessary to lead, to follow, and to solve problems. Because we serve together in this process of discovery, a strong team begins to form that is built on trust and understanding.

## TEAMS ARE IMPORTANT

Regardless of the size of the congregation, building teams for ministry with young people is an important structural piece to establishing a sustainable ministry. (See Figure 1.) I'll go into detail about each of the teams and explain why they are necessary. A dynamic ministry with young people should include the following teams:

**1. The Youth Council,
   a.k.a. the Youth Leadership Team**

**2. The Youth Ministry Team**

**3. The Parent Advisory Team**

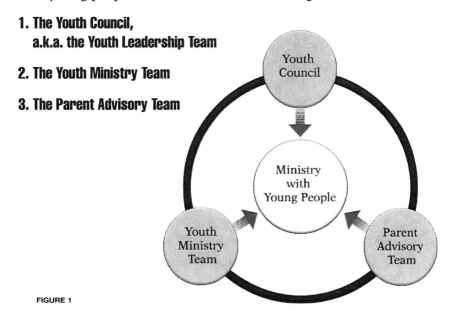

FIGURE 1

67

## The Youth Council, a.k.a. the Youth Leadership Team

The United Methodist Church advocates that all UMC youth ministries have a functioning Youth Council. The membership of the council should be comprised of at least three-fourths youth. The remaining council members include at least one young adult, the youth ministry coordinator, any youth serving beyond the local church in ministry leadership, and other adults serving on United Methodist-related youth ministry councils. The purpose of this council is to help vision, plan, develop, and evaluate the ministry with youth. Regardless of your denominational affiliation, this is a great place to start in engaging youth in leadership. The youth members are either self-selected or, in some cases, elected by their peers. This team of leaders, also known as the Youth Leadership Team, when engaged fully in its role, has the ability to design a dynamic and vibrant ministry with young people.

As young people serve as part of this team and are mentored by committed adults, they begin to learn that leadership is more than a position, it's a lifestyle. Additionally, making room for youth to lead is an essential part of fostering a culture of call. A culture of call develops as teens utilize their gifts and skills and they have the opportunity to discover how God has uniquely designed them for ministry in the world, whether that be as a clergy or as a layperson. A ministry that engages, equips, and empowers young people through leadership opportunities will experience vibrancy regardless of the number of people engaged in the ministry.

Todd shares how serving on the Youth Council while in high school was a life-changing experience.

> It felt weird at first. As a young person, only fifteen or sixteen years old, I was serving alongside people who had master's degrees and PhDs, people who had been serving in churches for decades, and people with mile-long resumés while I was just a junior in high school trying to balance homework, a summer job, and now opportunities to serve in ministry.

These experiences, however, taught me more about ministry than any other experience thus far. The clergy and lay leaders I worked with didn't see me as under them, but with them. They worked with me as another human in ministry, not a kid. This attitude from those I worked with helped me to understand how ministry really looked. It allowed me to have the experiences of success and failure, and to get a hands-on feel for how it would be to one day be a youth leader, an ordained minister, or a conference director. Being allowed to work alongside adult leaders in the church also gave me a sense of confidence. I felt as though I was trusted with the "big tasks," and that I wasn't being treated as a kid. Those around took my call to ministry seriously, and allowed me to explore that call through opportunities in ministry that truly tested my determination, and helped me to later on reflect and discern what exactly God may be calling me to. If it wasn't for the adult lay and clergy leaders who empowered me as a high schooler to take leaps of faith, try new things, and serve in big ways, I would not be serving in the capacity I am today, or be prepared for the ministries I serve now.

## The Youth Ministry Team

The Youth Ministry Team consists of the adults who are leading and executing the church's youth ministry. This includes the person designated as the youth minister as well as other adults from the congregation who share in responsibility for the youth ministry. This team should be diverse in gender, ethnicity if possible, and life stage. The Youth Ministry Team partners with the Youth Council to implement the plans for ministry that will help the group accomplish her mission.

Often the Youth Ministry Team is one of the most overlooked and underutilized teams in ministry. However this team is essential to the faith formation of your teens. It's more than just a safe sanctuary or health and safety requirement to have multiple adults serving in ministry with young people. As we will go into deeper detail in the chapter on discipleship, young people need multiple mentors speaking and modeling faith.

For many, this approach will require a change in thinking. Gone are the days of the hero-leader paradigm where one person makes it all happen while everyone else assists. In Chapter 2 we talked about the pitfalls of the pastor-centered model of leadership in the church. This hero-leader youth minister is an extension of that concept. While it is necessary to have a point person who is tasked with the organizational components of the ministry, it is equally necessary to have a team of committed adults who are willing to build relationships with young people.

Contrary to widely held belief, teens don't care how old their leaders are. A large number of young people who were interviewed as part of a study called Growing Young by the Fuller Youth Institute said that young people want their ministry leaders to offer authenticity more than being young and flashy.[4]

That has been our experience as well. The churches who have participated in the Smaller Church Youth Ministry Initiative and are thriving are represented by youth ministry volunteers from a wide range of ages. The takeaway from this is that teens' primary need from your church is to be both challenged and supported in their faith formation rather than be a "cool" place with "cool people." There are people in your congregation who desire a place to serve but might be overlooked if "young and flashy" are your criteria for a youth ministry leader.

As you build your team, clearly you will need people who can teach biblical truth in a way that will engage young people in faith discussions. That said, not everyone is gifted to teach. You will also need people with other gifts and strengths as well, such as organization, creativity, leading worship, and so forth. Well-defined ministry descriptions will be one of the best gifts you can give to your adult leaders as it will help them understand clearly what is being asked of them and how they will be able to use their gifts and strengths to their best abilities in relationship with the rest of the team. Once your team is recruited and equipped, it must be free to lead in order to function at its best.

### The Parent Advisory Team

The Parent Advisory Team is essential to building a youth ministry that lasts. This team will consist of parents and/or guardians of young people involved in your church's youth ministry. It should be made of no less than three but no more than eight persons. Think of this team as the PTO for your ministry. PTO stands for Parent Teacher Organization. PTOs support and advocate for the needs of the teachers and students in their school. The Parent Advisory Team serves as a support group and an advocate for the youth ministry in your congregation. This team can assist with fundraising, provide food for activities and events, and help with administrative work such as creating the youth ministry calendar of important school and community events. Additionally, this team can help connect parents with one another and the church and engage parents who want to be involved but are not able to be a part of the weekly ministry team.

## DEFINING ROLES IS NECESSARY

Every team member needs a role with clearly defined responsibilities and expectations. Consider some of the following roles and recommended sub-teams that veteran youth minister and writer Gavin Richardson defines as necessary for ministry with young people.[5] As you build your ministry, it might not be possible or necessary for you to include every one of the following options. Some of these roles and teams consist of adults only; some can be a combination of youth and adults working collaboratively. Try to include as many different people as possible. Avoid allowing any one individual to take on more than two roles at the same time.

As you determine what is necessary, allow your mission to guide you in selecting those components needed to reach it. Every role is to function in collaboration with the Youth Ministry Team to ensure alignment with the overall mission.

## Youth Council

A. **Youth Council Chair or President:** The Chair or President of the Youth Council is a youth chosen by his or her peers. This person will work with the lead youth minister to create the agenda for Youth Council meetings. This person will lead the meetings with assistance from the lead youth minister.

B. **Youth Council Vice Chair or Vice President:** The Vice Chair or Vice President of the Youth Council is a youth chosen by his or her peers. This person will assist the Youth Council President with the Youth Council meetings.

C. **Youth Council Secretary:** The Secretary of the Youth Council is a youth chosen by his or her peers. This person will take the roll and keep the minutes of the Youth Council meeting.

D. **Youth Finance Coordinator:** I don't know very many youth minister types who are great at handling finances. However, there is someone in your congregation who has the necessary skills. Money management or the lack thereof is one of the major concerns most church leaders have with their youth minister. Invite someone to be on the team who can help with these responsibilities. It's a good idea that this person also be a member of the church's finance committee so that the person has the ability to speak on the ministry's behalf. Having an advocate in the room will help solve misunderstandings and promote transparency. This person will meet with the Youth Council to formulate budgets for both monthly and regular ministry activities while keeping track of expenses and deposits from event registrations. The Youth Finance Coordinator partners with the Big Event Coordinator and Youth Fundraising Coordinator.

E. **Youth Communications Team:** This team will coordinate and create the marketing pieces to communicate the big events, fundraisers, and ongoing ministry activity. The team will be sure that pictures are taken and videos created to share the story of the ministry with the congregation. The Youth Communications Team will work cooperatively with the Youth Ministry Team and Youth Council to ensure that upcoming teaching themes are promoted to the entire congregation. The team should consist of youth and adults.

F. **Youth Fundraising Coordinator:** This person will plan and facilitate the fundraisers needed to support your church's youth ministry throughout the year. The person will handle logistics and recruit volunteers necessary for fundraising events to meet the goals set in cooperation with the Youth Council and the Youth Finance Coordinator. This person is also a part of the Parent Advisory Team.

## Youth Ministry Team

A. **Youth Minister(s):** Person(s) in this role will serve on the Youth Ministry Team. They will be involved in leading the regular ministry gatherings, a.k.a. Youth Group. They will teach or coordinate the lesson, the activities, and the other components of the regular meeting time.

B. **Sunday School Teacher:** The Sunday School Teacher should be someone who has the ability to teach in a way that helps teens engage in their own faith formation. While the Sunday School Teachers may not come to all the youth ministry gatherings on a regular basis, they should be expected to participate in at least one activity outside of

Sunday school each month as a way to extend support, nurture, care, and relationship with both those who attend Sunday school and those who do not.

C. **Small Group Leader:** If you utilize small groups in your ministry, you'll want to have strong Small Group Leaders. In the smaller membership church, small groups might be formed by separating genders or you might separate them based on high school or middle school grade levels. The Small Group Leaders are important mentors for faith development. In some churches, Small Group Leaders will stay with the same young people from middle school through high school graduation. They provide another necessary point of contact essential to faith development.

D. **Youth Worship Team:** This team is best comprised of adults and youth together whose job it is to create worship experiences for youth group and events such as retreats. This team would include oversight of visual design, dance, art, instruments, singers, and more. In the church where I attend, Miss Bea has become one of our best youth ministers by connecting her strengths and passions with those of many of our young people simply by offering a youth orchestra.

## Parent Advisory Team(s)

A. **Big Event Coordinator:** *Big* is a relative term, but coordinating events while trying to lead a youth ministry is difficult. That is why this person is so vital. The Big Event Coordinator will handle the details associated with retreats, mission trips, and camps. This person will make sure that housing reservations are made, travel arrangements are figured out, additional volunteers are recruited, and registration of attendees is handled. As part of the responsibilities, this person will create a notebook that is a central storage location for all things related to each specific event.

B. **Confirmation Support Team:** Sometimes smaller membership churches choose to not offer faith confirmation training because they don't believe they have enough young people to warrant offering the program. What if your church decided to offer confirmation training for your community by connecting with other smaller membership congregations in your area to provide this formative training? The Confirmation Support Team's purpose is to help coordinate the resources and people necessary to offer an effective and dynamic confirmation experience. This team will coordinate the persons who will serve as mentors during the confirmation program. This team will serve as Small Group Leaders for students as they transition into the youth ministry. This team will help coordinate a memory maker activity to celebrate the transition of younger students into the ministry.

C. **Youth Kitchen Team:** This team will consist of adults and youth who through coordination with the Parent Advisory Team prepare the meal and/or snacks for regular youth ministry gatherings, including Sunday mornings. They will help clean up after the fellowship/meal time is completed, and they will coordinate the purchase of items needed for fellowship/meal times. The coordinator of this team will serve on the Parent Advisory Team and on the Youth Council.

D. **Youth Prayer Team:** This might just be the most important team your ministry will form. The cool thing about this team is that its only requirement for membership is that the team members pray for all parts of the ministry with young people. This means that there aren't any age requirements to be a part of the team. It also means that the members of the team don't have to be present at youth group meetings in order to participate. This provides the opportunity for the eldest members of your congregation to fully participate. It provides opportunities for those members of your congregation who might be unable to leave their homes to participate as well. The coordinator of the team will be a part of the Youth Council.

# ENGAGING OLDER ADULTS

By the year 2030, it is projected that 21 percent of the U.S. population will be eighteen years old and under and 21 percent of the population will be sixty-five and older.[6] This creates a great opportunity for the church to be intentional about connecting every young person with at least one older adult in our congregations. One of the ways I've seen this happen is at the church I attend. Each spring, the youth group sponsors a "Senior Prom" with the local retirement and assisted living home. During this activity, young and old wear their best clothes, spend time in conversation, share a meal together, and dance! The joy that is generated for both age groups is enormous. The stories that are shared are priceless. Many thriving smaller membership churches currently do these kinds of things. The more we can create opportunities for young people and older folks to participate together in life and ministry, the better the church and the world will be.

## Rev. Michael Williams' story

Rev. Michael Williams is the pastor of West End United Methodist Church in Nashville, Tennessee. West End is one of the larger congregations in the Tennessee Conference. Michael is a well-known writer, speaker, and storyteller. Both of his daughters served in leadership roles in their local churches as well as on the Conference Council on Youth Ministry for the Tennessee Conference. As I was sharing with Michael about this book project, he excitedly asked if he could share his story of the impact that a smaller congregation has had on his life.

> In 1960 my father moved our trailer on to a half-acre plot on Old Palmyra Road in Montgomery County. Shortly thereafter we began to attend the Antioch Methodist Church, which at that time was one of four churches on the Antioch Charge. I was baptized at the close of the confirmation class taught by our pastor, a Vanderbilt Divinity School student named Arnold Vorster, who had been born in South Africa. My mother had grown up Baptist, so I had not been baptized as an infant, and I requested baptism by immersion. So, on a Sunday afternoon I was baptized by a student pastor from South Africa in the baptistery of First Christian Church in Clarksville, Tennessee, with members of my home congregation in attendance.

> Because there were four congregations to be served, the preacher would lead worship only three Sundays a month in each congregation. On the alternate Sunday we had Sunday School Assembly before adjourning to Sunday school classes. During those assemblies, Scripture would be read, prayers said, announcements made, and a hymn or two sung. As a young person I was encouraged to serve as one of the Scripture readers. My experiences as a youth in this small membership church formed who I am today.

> In 1965 Jerry Hilton was appointed to be our pastor. While our pastors took part in our formation as young people, the majority of our learning to be disciples came from laypersons. My Sunday school teacher was Wayne Mittler, whose preparation for each class demonstrated his respect for the material he was to teach as well as those of us who had come to learn. Our Methodist Youth Fellowship leaders were sisters, Miss Anna Belle Powers and Miss Alice Coke. Though both sisters were married, we still referred to them as Miss

Anna Belle and Miss Alice. Both women encouraged (a more accurate term might be coerced) me into taking a leadership role in the youth group. I learned to plan and lead programs, which required that I learn something about interpreting Scripture as well as speaking before the young people from all four churches on the charge. Then when I was sixteen, an MYF member from another church on the charge nominated me to serve as president of the Sub-District MYF and I was elected. This gave me the opportunity to grow in both discipleship and leadership within the Tennessee Conference.

Arnold Vorster baptized me. Jerry Hilton first suggested to my parents and to me that God might be calling me to ordained ministry. I learned more than I can say from the preaching of both of these pastors, but it was Mr. Mittler, Miss Anna Belle, and Miss Alice who gave me the opportunity to grow as a disciple and a leader. As of 2016, I have been an ordained member of the Tennessee Conference for forty-two years, in large part because of the love and opportunities afforded me by a small but faithful congregation.

# STEPHANIE'S RESPONSE

Have I told you that my hubby and I have seven kids and twenty-plus grandkids? Just this morning, I had to review the list for my hubby and who belongs to whom. Craziness, right? My life has always been about multiple numbers of kids around me. I have eight other siblings, then I go into youth ministry where you're never anywhere alone, and then we have this large family. Double craziness!

So a few times a year, Casa Caro becomes the home of Camp Grandma—where my "youth pastor" self meets my "grandma" self and collides with my "VBS director" self. Different combos of grandkids descend upon our home for time with Grandma and Grandpa. We have one Camp Grandma every summer, plus one or two special holiday camps most years. Each week has a theme with activities, crafts, food, and so on, all matching the theme. Examples from the past are A Year's Worth of Holidays, Water Wonders, Easter Movie Madness, Under the Sea, and Texas Traditions.

Here's a not-very-well-kept secret: It's WAY more fun being a grandparent than a parent. For me, I know the kids are going back home to their parents after Camp Grandma! Also, there's something to be said that as a grandparent, your legs may not be as young as they used to be … but you're wiser; work smarter, not harder; and you generally have more money to make things happen than you did when your kids were young. This year? I hired an intern!

As I write this, I am still cleaning up from Camp Grandma Summer 2016. I put the g-kids on a plane a week ago and closed the books on another house full of noise and adventure. I'd mark it a success … yet something was different this year. The kids are getting older and my old bag of tricks didn't work like they had in the past. Not every idea I had planned was met with the same former years' delight. It took me about a day and a half into camp week to realize that I'd better make a few adaptive changes. This year's crop of g-kids needed more input. Appetites had changed. Social media and electronics played a more visible role.

At first I thought I'd ignore it and then I remembered: I invited them here to enjoy this. They weren't forced to be here. For this to work and if I'm the smart grandma I think I am, I need to keep it relevant. So we made a few changes, set a few limits, scratched a few other ideas, allowed them leadership input. It worked mostly, a few things didn't, no police/fire department calls were needed, and this year's blow-up pool actually survived still holding water till the end with only one patch (a record for Camp Grandma).

OK, there's a point: As students age into your youth program from the children's ministry world, they need an increased number of ways to keep interested and ownership in what's happening. Doing everything the same old way probably won't work anymore. They need a say, input. They need opportunities to try and fail. But they really don't want to do it all on their own, either. Besides, completely student-led isn't biblical.

A good climate for allowing them to lead begins with you. You have to set aside what used to work. You have to move toward their "new" world, not ask them to function in your "old" world. The most successful climate around youth is one that figures out what each teenager has to offer, their giftedness today for the ministry needs today. Not the way it used to be done; not the way it will be done. Striking an attitude of adaptive change that moves with the needs of each youth ministry as it ebbs and flows with each new school year is what will make relevant leadership happen.

My final two cents on this (and it may not be popular with some die-hard structure/process people): I'm not a fan of traditional roles in setting up student leadership teams. Holding elections seems to set up a popularity process that doesn't always lend itself to actually choosing the best student leaders to lead in their best way.

What if instead you advertised what the student leadership team will be responsible for and just invite students to come and do what they're interested in? Or better yet, what if you invited anyone who wanted to be on the leadership team, evaluated who showed up, and let the program follow the people? Even better yet—what if you just naturally (with a little intentionality behind the scenes) infused leadership opportunities into everything in your ministry? You know, met students where they're at, develop them along, bringing them up to be their part of the Body?

# DISCUSSION QUESTIONS FOR CHAPTER 4: LEADING

1. Who are some current young leaders in your congregation? How have they shown leadership in the church, and how could they be nurtured to grow and serve as leaders in the church and youth ministry?

2. How is your congregation overall cultivating a Matthew 4:19 disciple-making culture ("Come, follow me ... and I'll show you how to fish for people.")? How can you envision this culture shaping your youth ministry? Or, how can this culture be established in the youth ministry and take hold through the entire congregation?

3. Describe the ways you see the lifestyle of leadership in your life and the lives of your team? How could you develop a Youth Council and teach the importance of a leader lifestyle in your youth ministry?

4. The connection between older adults and young people can create opportunities for mutual spiritual growth, and mentorship for the young person. How can you establish these intergenerational connections in your local church?

# CHAPTER 5

# IT'S MORE THAN SAFE SANCTUARIES

The United Methodist Church adopted a resolution at the 1996 General Conference that began the process of developing policies, procedures, training, and resources for reducing the risk of child sexual abuse in the church. As a result, The United Methodist Church has been at the forefront of helping clergy and laity understand the necessity of keeping ministry safe.

A component of this resolution was the development of the Safe Sanctuary program. "Safe Sanctuaries is an overt expression in making congregations safe places where children, youth, and elders may experience the abiding love of God and fellowship within the community of faith."[1] A Safe Sanctuary policy along with specific procedures needed for implementation is an essential component of a strong ministry with young people. It takes more than just implementing a strong Safe Sanctuary policy to reduce the risk. Equally important is an understanding of how to live and serve while in relationship with others. This is known as Healthy Boundaries. Safe Sanctuaries and Healthy Boundaries combined together allow us to live and serve in healthy relationships that connect and reveal God's love for all of us.

## WHY?

One of the most common reactions I receive when I talk to churches, especially smaller congregations, is the question, "But why do we need this when we're already safe?" This question often comes because they have formed the perception that implementing the components to create a safe ministry will be restricting and challenging. Concerned already about a small pool of volunteers, they fear that implementing these policies will reduce the number of potential volunteers even more. Additionally, some have the opinion that this process will limit their ability to do ministry because it will cause them to be more focused on safety than ministry. Still others believe that nothing bad could ever happen in their congregation because "we're all family here."

## Rise in sexual abuse

We live in a broken world. The incidence of sexual abuse continues to rise even while law enforcement, community organizations, and religious groups have worked diligently to educate and create policies to reduce the risk. While many instances of child sexual abuse are reported, most are not. In 2010, the U.S. Department of Health and Human Services Children's Bureau reported that 9.2 percent of victimized children were sexually assaulted.[2] Studies by the director of the Crimes Against Children Research Center reveal the following statistics:

- One in five girls and one in twenty boys are victims of child sexual abuse;

- Self-report studies show that 20 percent of adult females and 5–10 percent of adult males recall a childhood sexual assault or sexual abuse incident;

- During a one-year period in the U.S., 16 percent of youth ages fourteen to seventeen had been sexually victimized;

- Over the course of their lifetimes, 28 percent of U.S. youth ages fourteen to seventeen had been sexually victimized;

- Children are most vulnerable to child sexual abuse between the ages of seven and thirteen.[3]

The Abel and Harlow Child Molestation Prevention Study released in 2001 and revised in 2002 revealed a startling fact. The study revealed that 93 percent of sex offenders describe themselves as "religious."[4] Dr. Ann Salter, author of the book *Predators, Pedophiles, Rapists, and other Sex Offenders,* shared one convicted child molester's words that should further confirm the need for church leaders to be diligent in keeping ministry safe:

> "I considered church people easy to fool . . . they have a trust that comes from being Christians. They tend to be better folks all around and seem to want to believe in the good that exists in people."[5]

Sadly, while the statistics are alarming and the stories are tragic, some church leaders still have difficulty realizing the necessity of policies and procedures that increase the vigilance of the congregation. While we see all people as children of God, even those who do harm, we have to become aware that while we want all to have the opportunity to participate in ministry, we also have a responsibility to protect all people. At the same time, this doesn't mean that all are able to serve in ministry with young people. Later in this chapter, I will go into deeper detail about the process of screening and educating ministry leaders.

## Need for safety

Abraham Maslow was an American psychologist who proposed in 1943 that humans are motivated by five basic needs. His Hierarchy of Needs is the framework we use for understanding the importance of a safe ministry environment. (See Figure 2.)

The foundational needs for all of us are physiological needs, which include food, water, shelter, and rest. Just above that level is the need for safety. Maslow identifies the combination of physiological needs and safety needs as "basic needs" for human psychosocial development.[6]

# Maslow's hierarchy of needs

**FIGURE 2**

Jesus understood this hierarchy of needs before Maslow ever devised it. In Matthew 18, Jesus revealed this importance:

> At that time the disciples came to Jesus and asked, "Who, then, is the greatest in the kingdom of heaven?"
>
> He called a little child to him, and placed the child among them. And he said: "Truly I tell you, unless you change and become like little children, you will never enter the kingdom of heaven. Therefore, whoever takes the lowly position of this child is the greatest in the kingdom of heaven. And whoever welcomes one such child in my name welcomes me.
>
> "If anyone causes one of these little ones—those who believe in me—to stumble, it would be better for them to have a large millstone hung around their neck and to be drowned in the depths of the sea."
>
> Matthew 18:1-6 (NIV)

A safe environment demonstrates you care. As you work to ensure that your ministries are safe, you will be more able to form a stronger community built on a deep commitment to relationships.

It is essential, then, that as we work to reduce the risk of harm in ministry, we understand that everyone, both young and old, has this need. David Kinnaman, president of the Barna Group, says:

Our research consistently shows that how a church treats children is one of the keys to drawing and retaining new families. Sadly, churches expose themselves to all kinds of potential problems by failing to screen the people who will have contact with and responsibility for the children of strangers during church events. There is a level of trust that newcomers as well as long-time members place in the capacity of a church to provide comprehensive care for their children.[7]

When my wife and I first attended Epworth United Methodist Church in 2001, we were new parents. Our daughter was just a few months old. Whether we realized it or not, from the moment we entered the sanctuary that first Sunday, we began assessing whether our need for safety was being realized. At the same time, we were doing that for our daughter. As we took our place on the back row, we took in the surroundings of that historic sanctuary. As people began to welcome us, one elderly woman chose to sit next to us. Throughout that service, not only did she make us feel welcome, but looking back, we also felt safe in that space with her. It was as if we were members of her family whom she had invited to join her on a Sunday for worship. She made us feel comfortable and she comforted our daughter. While the church offered a nursery, she didn't make us feel like we had to place our child there. Because of that awareness, we chose to come back to worship the next Sunday. A few months later, we joined the church. A few years later I became the youth minister there. All of the experiences over the past fifteen years at our church have occurred because we felt safe the first time we attended.

If you're having trouble recruiting people to serve in ministry, maybe you need to make sure their need for safety is being met. You might have met the basic need that would allow them to attend your church, but serving is another level of responsibility that requires another level of safety. In addition to clear role expectations, we want to know that we're not at risk of harm or liability while volunteering. The more training you can provide on the policies, procedures, and expectations of those serving and those they are serving, the more likely you will gain the volunteers you need. Creating a team of volunteers who are well trained, highly motivated, and willing to engage others will help your ministry accomplish its mission to create disciples of Jesus Christ for the transformation of the world.

One of the techniques I have used to help people understand why keeping ministry safe is essential is to get them talking about what concerns them. As they take time to contemplate and then verbalize their concerns, they begin to realize the necessity. I've seen the most ardent opponents of Safe Sanctuaries shift their opinion once they have taken time to truly reflect.

Here's how we do this in the cohort:

- Participants are divided into groups of three or four.

- They are given two or three minutes to create a list of the things in their church and ministry that have caused concern for them.

- As each group shares the list they have created, it becomes apparent that many of the concerns are shared by everyone else.

- We then spend time discussing solutions to those concerns.

I try to refrain from offering "expert advice" unless it's needed because most often they are able to offer an appropriate solution for the concern. Helping your church and team members understand "why" it is important to keep ministry safe is one of your first tasks. At the heart of the "why" are hearts and souls of the persons in your ministry. By focusing on creating a ministry that is a Safe Space, you will create a Sacred Space where transformation can occur for everyone.

## REDUCING RISK THROUGH SAFE SANCTUARIES

Now that you've discovered "why" it is important to keep ministry safe, let's talk about the components that contribute to reducing the risk. A great place to start is with a resource called *Safe Sanctuaries: Reducing the Risk of Abuse in the Church for Children and Youth*, by Joy Thornburg Melton. (For ordering information, look in the list of resources in the appendix section of this book.) The *Safe Sanctuaries* book includes background information, policies, and procedures that assure keeping ministry safe, and a process for developing your own church policy. As a bonus, there are sample job descriptions along with other sample forms you might need for ministry.

If you don't already have a church youth ministry risk management policy in place, here are several critical points that are important to consider to help you create your ministry's policy:

## FACES, ACTIVITIES, SPACES

As I train churches to develop policies and procedures for keeping ministry safe, I encourage them to think in terms of three basic categories:

1. Faces—the people who are serving, the people who are being served

2. Activities—the stuff the ministry does

3. Spaces—where ministry happens

As I like to say when I'm training folks, let's dive in.

### Faces

Churches should screen all of the adults who volunteer to work with children or youth in their congregations. Joy Thornburg Melton says: "Implementing a thorough screening process for the church's workers with [children and youth] and applying that process to all workers (paid and volunteer, clergy and lay) will go a long way toward demonstrating that the church has taken reasonable actions to protect its [children and youth]."[8] There are at least three components to the screening process that I recommend:

1. A written application

2. An interview

3. A national criminal records background check

**A written application:** I recommend that you have an application they can complete that asks some basic questions about why they feel called to serve in your ministry. Be sure to include a job description for the role you're asking them to serve in, with some specific questions related to their willingness to complete that role. Also include any other specific expectations related to interpersonal relationships, social media, and interaction with the young people in the church and ministry.

**An interview:** Follow the written application with an interview with you, the pastor, and/or another previously approved adult volunteer serving in the ministry. If they are unwilling to participate in completing the application and/or refuse to commit to the interview, you wouldn't want them on your team anyway. During the interview, you'll review the application questions and ask for clarification of answers if needed.

**A national criminal records background check:** As a final component of the screening process, it is necessary for potential volunteers to submit to a national criminal records background check conducted by a professional service. There are a number of companies from which to choose. I recommend you utilize a company that provides its services through the Internet. This will make the process move more quickly and you won't have to store sensitive information at your location. Most services are now designed in such a way that you send a request that generates an e-mail to the applicant. The applicant completes the requested information asked by the company. The check is conducted, and you'll get a response quickly identifying any level of concern.

There is a cost involved for the check. Some ministries choose to pay that fee and others ask the applicant to assume the cost. After you receive your report, be sure to take time to review any concerns that the company found. Some concerns may require you to have a conversation with the applicant. While background checks are technically valid for five years, best practice recommends a new check every two to three years or when a physical change of address occurs.

While background checks are necessary and often required by your church's insurance company, keep in mind that they do not guarantee each person with a clean report is not an offender. Law enforcement estimates that 88 percent of sexual abuse is never reported.[9] This means potentially only one in ten persons will have a background check flagging them for conviction of abuse of any kind.

Although such screening seems tedious, Melton argues it is necessary:

> Abuse prevention and risk-reduction policies and procedures are essential for every congregation, not only for the protection and safety of our youth and children … but also for our volunteer and paid workers with children and youth. Local congregations differ in the ways they engage in ministry with [young people]. Therefore, each congregation's need for prevention policies and guidelines will be somewhat different from the others.
>
> The gospel calls us to be engaged in ministry with [young people]. We must not allow the risks to undermine or stop our ministry. Rather, we must
>
> - acknowledge the risks and develop a practical plan to reduce them;

- take steps to prevent harm to our [young people and workers];

- continue to answer the gospel's imperative to be in ministry with [young people], making a difference in their lives.[10]

If you choose to utilize young adults, ages nineteen to twenty, it won't be sufficient or beneficial to conduct a background check with this age group. The reason is that they have not had enough "adult" years of life beyond the restriction on juvenile records. In this case, as with other age groups, requesting and checking references is a vital tool in the screening process. It is also best practice that persons leading ministry with young people be at least five years older than the oldest person in the ministry. If you utilize young adults who don't meet this criteria in ministry, be aware of where you are allowing them to serve. One recommendation is they be allowed to serve in ministry with children or middle school youth but not high school age youth. If this is not avoidable, then they should be paired with adults who do meet the age difference requirements.

**The Two Adult Rule.** This is a simple requirement where no fewer than two adults are present at all times during any activity connected to the church's ministry with young people. If those two adults are not related, you'll reduce risk even more. It is recommended that the genders of the adults present correspond with the genders of the young people present. Simply put, if there are female young people present, be sure there is a female adult, and if male young people present, a male adult will be present. Often I'm asked about specific scenarios that apply to the Two Adult Rule. Questions like: "What about Sunday school?" Answer: Two Adults; "What about Bible study?" Answer: Two Adults; "What about youth group?" You guessed it, Two Adults.

Smaller congregations often push back that they don't have enough people available to make this happen and they ask: "What then?"

If you work to build a team of volunteers who understand "why" it is important, I believe you'll not have this problem. That's my first answer. If you don't have enough adults to meet the Two Adult Rule, best practice would recommend you combine classes or hold ministry in a space that can be shared by other groups (more on spaces later). This is often in a fellowship hall or quite possibly the sanctuary. Some churches might utilize persons who are known as Roamers. These persons are trained and background-checked adults who move from room to room to observe and assist as needed when meeting the Two Adult Rule is difficult to achieve. Ministries that work to build a team of adults who can serve in roles that assist to meet the Two Adult Rule will see a greater reduction of risk for both the young people and the ministry leaders in the ministry.

## Activities

The needs for reducing risk are also determined by the types of activities the ministry does. The activity your group is involved in will help determine the necessary adult-to-youth ratio needed to ensure safety. While the Two Adult Rule should always apply, the number of youth accompanying those two adults might require you to invite more adults to help. The general rule is that you should always have at least one adult for every eight youth. So that means you would have at least two adults for every sixteen youth. As your group grows in number of young people, you should also grow the number of adults volunteering in your ministry. Some activities such as mission trips have a smaller ratio of adults to youth such as one adult for every six youth. The change in ratio is meant to help provide a deeper level of risk reduction. Another factor that may create smaller ratio of adults to youth would be the age of the youth involved. Generally speaking, the younger the child, the more adults required. This is because younger children are particularly vulnerable and require more care and attention. Don't forget to make sure that the genders of your adults match the genders represented in your ministry.

It is necessary to have all of the participants in any activity (weekly gatherings, events, and so forth) complete a health/release form each year. Be sure to keep a set of these forms in a secure location in the church office. If you're able, you might want to scan each member's form and store them electronically. When your group attends a retreat offered by your conference or another organization that requires copies of release forms, simply make copies of the originals to submit with your registration.

When you travel, take a set of these forms with you. I recommend that you have a complete set in each vehicle on the trip. Chances are you'll never need them, but in the event of an accident or another emergency, you'll be glad you did. Some third-party providers such as mission companies or outdoor adventure activities may require you to complete a custom form specific to their organization. Be sure to coordinate with these groups before heading out in case you need your young people's parents to complete the forms. It won't be a great experience for you to arrive at the activity and not have this completed.

## Spaces

In a smaller congregation or in times where multiple adults might be overwhelming to the ministry need, you can still make adjustments to keep ministry safe. In ministry involving one or more youth with only one adult, consider meeting:

- at a coffee shop or a fast-food restaurant where you can get a beverage and hold a discussion;

- outdoors for a service project;

- on the swing at a community playground;

- outside the church on the lawn or a bench;

- for a walk around the neighborhood;

- at the home of a youth with a parent in the next room while the doors are open;

- at your home with your spouse or another family member nearby. Never meet in a bedroom; instead, use the kitchen table or the living room.

- at a picnic table in the park for a Bible study;

- in the fellowship hall while another group meets nearby but out of listening range.

As you think about the spaces where ministry takes place, what adjustments might be needed to reduce risk in those areas? Some questions to ask include:

- Can this activity be held in a more visible location so that risk can be reduced?

- When standing at the door of the room where ministry is happening, are there clear sight lines for all parts of the room?

- Does the door have a window in it? If not, I should leave the door open when in use.

- After I finish using this part of the church and participants are gone, can I lock doors to ensure the area is unoccupied unless in use?

- Are there clear action plans established in the event of an emergency such as a fire, inclement weather, or other action requiring special attention?

- What about cyberspace?

**Cyberspace.** As you are aware, we live in a highly digital world. So this means one of the spaces we have to consider in reducing risk is the Internet. It's almost impossible in today's highly connected world to restrict access to the Internet. Research shows at least 73 percent of teens (thirteen to seventeen) have smartphones.[11]

This means they have access to the Internet virtually 24/7. So it's not as easy as saying that the answer to reducing risk is to simply put firewalls on Internet access points. To reduce risk in today's ever-changing digital world, we have to educate young people and their caregivers on safe and appropriate usage.

Educating parents and caregivers might just be our biggest challenge, but it's one youth ministry leaders need to face. Kevin Alton wrote in an article for the Institute for Youth Ministry at Princeton Theological Seminary's blog that parents sometimes tend to range across two extremes: too open or too controlling. He says:

> It's one thing to give them their space; it's another to give them *all* of the space ... It's not about control and it's not even all about protection ... Parents don't necessarily need to kick their children off of social media, but they must be willing to walk with them."[12]

I get it. I'm a parent of two teenagers. Parenting is the most difficult but most rewarding job I get to experience each day. If I'm not careful, living in a digitally connected age can make it more challenging than rewarding. My children are unique in the way they interact digitally, but they are also very similar. I think it is because of the way that my wife and I talk with them about social media while also having a presence with them on social media. We regularly talk with them about appropriate use of the Internet. My daughter will tell you that I'm a bit overbearing. I'm really not, though. There's a difference between being proactive through presence and being reactive because of absence. Because of that presence and openness, our daughter will ask us when she doesn't know someone who has asked to "friend" her on Facebook. We can determine together who and why this person would request such a connection. This didn't come without some tough discussions on what is appropriate and not appropriate to like, share, or post. We've not perfected the process by any means, but we've been willing to learn and talk about safe interaction in this space.

Not all parents of teens in your ministry will have an awareness of what their children do and don't do online. That is why offering opportunities for training parents and their children together can be an important step for reducing the risk of harm in this space. There are some great resources available that help youth ministry leaders and parents navigate this ever-changing digital space. Your local police department can also be a great resource for training and discussion about cyber safety. (For a list of resources, look in the appendix section of this book.)

## REDUCING THE RISK THROUGH PERSONAL BOUNDARIES
Boundaries are essential because they define where one person ends and the other begins. They help define how we will interact with each other and what we should and shouldn't expect from each other. We make assumptions all the time; most often it's that everyone understands what it means to have appropriate boundaries. Sadly, most don't. It's not that they intentionally seek to violate another's boundaries; it's just that most often clear boundaries were not formed or agreed upon at the start. While it's important for ministry leaders to spend time developing clear boundaries for how they will serve in ministry, it's equally important for life outside of ministry.

**Knowing yourself.** An important responsibility you have in reducing risk is knowing yourself. One of the most powerful processes I experienced in forming boundaries for myself was during an exercise on creating my Personal Vocational Values. During this process I was forced to examine four areas:

1. the things it appears I value by my actions

2. the things that I profess I value

3. the things that have defined me

4. the things that I want to define me

As I spent time contemplating each of those areas, I realized that I had not provided a clear definition of my boundaries for others or most importantly myself. The way that I was living my life and leading in ministry were in conflict with what I professed I valued. Because of this mismatch, which I was perpetuating, I realized that others were treating me the way I was treating myself. While I talked about the importance of Sabbath and life balance, I was over-scheduled, overcommitted, and always available. I was suffering from the difficulty many of us in ministry face of not wanting to appear unavailable. I had bought into the unwritten rule (it's a false one) that implies ministry leaders must be available 24/7.

As a result of this realization, I immediately defined a boundary that would exhibit what I said I valued. I arranged my schedule so that I would have at least one day during the week where I was "unavailable." Most weeks I am able to set that day as Monday. However, sometimes I divide an equivalent amount of time throughout the week or find another day, especially one that would allow me to spend time with my family.

I also stopped working at home when I needed to be present with my family. After examining our family calendar, I determine when it is appropriate to work a little later to complete a project. I stop answering e-mails and phone calls that could wait until the next work day. As with any new skill, I have to practice it daily for it to be sustainable. At first, I failed more than I succeeded.

## Personal Vocational Values

Here is my list of my Personal Vocational Values:

1. Sabbath is vital. A ruthless commitment to Sabbath is necessary for my sustainability and health.

2. My family is my focus. I desire to be involved and present in the lives of my wife and children. Time spent with them is more valuable than time in office.

3. I am fueled by opportunities that challenge me to my fullest potential. I won't settle for experiences or situations in my professional life that expect less. I want to continually grow and lean more fully into God's call for my life.

4. I am not afraid of purpose-driven change. I thrive best in spaces where there is movement toward a preferred future instead of celebrating or lamenting the past.

5. I am fueled by relationships. I am energized by strong personal relationships in my personal and professional life.

6. Space for creativity is nonnegotiable. I need to create for the sake of creating. I desire opportunities to create new experiences for spiritual and personal growth.

I have found that by developing my Personal Vocational Values I am able to define what my "yes" will be and what my "no" will be. As I evaluate next steps and new opportunities, I pull out this list. I feel more confident in the decisions I make because of this understanding. When I am experiencing frustration or uncertainty, I can easily identify which of those items are not being met. This realization allows me to make decisions on what needs to change for realignment. I am healthier in ministry and in life because of this discovery. What about you?

**Self care.** A key aspect of boundary maintenance that I had to discover was the importance of self care. As I mentioned earlier, the process of defining my boundaries through discovering my Personal Vocational Values was an important factor in my physical, emotional, and spiritual health. If we're not taking care of our self physically, emotionally, and spiritually, it's difficult to live out Deuteronomy 6:5 (NIV): "Love the LORD your God with all your heart and with all your soul and with all your strength."

Jesus understood the need for developing healthy boundaries. One of the best resources I have found that helped me understand how

Jesus set boundaries was from a blog by Bill Gaultiere written back in 1998 on the website *www.soulshepherding.org*. He writes:

> It's no wonder we overdo in ministry, get worn out, and even burnout! Jesus had far more stress, far more pressure, and far more responsibility than any of us and yet he remained relaxed, joyful, and generous with people. He models and mediates for us living in God's rhythms of grace.[13]

I often hear youth ministry leaders talk about putting in seventy- to eighty-hour work weeks like that's a badge of honor. Truth is, they are on their way to crash and burn. This is one of the key areas where youth ministry leaders need to lead smarter, not harder. Spending time building a team of adults who are willing to share the load of relational ministry is critical in building a sustainable ministry. Spending time empowering parents to take on some of the logistical components of the ministry will also reduce the strain on time the ministry leader faces. Look back at Chapter 4 on leading if you need a reminder. I suggest you also take a look at how Jesus led. Jesus led smarter, he developed a team who could share in the ministry, and he realized that in order to do the hard things, he had to be emotionally, physically, and spiritually fit.

That is why when I read Bill's article I felt it was too important not to share. In fact, I've made it a part of the trainings I provide on the importance of boundaries. What is revealed is that even the Son of God, Jesus, understood that in his humanness he had limitations that had to be considered if he were to fulfill all that God had planned for him. I encourage you to take a look at Bill's work.

When we believe that we are to sacrifice ourselves to save others, we're about to cross boundaries. We don't have to be someone's savior—Jesus has already taken on that role. Our role is to maintain healthy boundaries so that we will be able to connect those whom God has entrusted to us into a deeper relationship with their Creator.

Tending to our souls is best done when we're in covenant with others. A way to do this is form a group with others in ministry either on your team or in your community and covenant to provide accountability and support for each other. John Wesley, the founder of the Methodist movement, suggested that small groups (he called them class meetings) should start off each meeting with the question: "How is it with your soul?" It's a tough question for most of us to answer because it's not a surface level question like "How are you?" We can easily answer superficial questions with quick answers, but if we truly open ourselves to the possibilities of revealing our inner self, God's grace and transformation will pour in. We all have likely had experiences where everything superficially was going wonderfully well but at the same time our souls were in turmoil. If we are to truly live a life where boundaries are clear, we must make time for soul care a priority as it is key to self care. So, "How is it with your soul?"

**You and power.** The risk of not clarifying your boundaries is dangerous. While not all boundary violations warrant criminal charges, some might. Just take a moment and do a quick search on Google. Start with "youth minister mugshots." While I don't know every one of the stories represented by the images in your search, I do know a few. Sadly, some of those represented by the pictures were people who saw the opportunity as a minister with young people as an invitation to victimize children. However, some of those offenders were different even though the outcome was the same. Because they failed to establish clear boundaries, they made choices that resulted in tragic circumstances. Don't get me wrong here, I'm not defending them or shifting responsibility from them. At the same time, had they spent time clearly defining themselves and their boundaries, I don't think they would have made the choices they did. The reality is along the way they said YES to many things that they should have said NO to and each "bad yes" compounded another. The result was devastating.

We run the same risk when we believe we don't have power. I once heard it said that youth ministers are often the most arrogant and most fragile persons in the room. We try to balance being in control while making sure people like us. It's a challenging act to balance. Because of that, we have to understand the power dynamics involved in ministry. Your power comes from the position you hold and/or the resources you possess. With that power you have the ability to help or hurt someone else. When we believe we are the only one who can help solve someone else's problem, we're setting ourselves up to cross a boundary. While our hearts might tell us to fix the situation, we must make sure that we have the correct resources to do so. In all cases our role in ministry is to connect them more deeply with God through their relationship with Jesus Christ. We must allow those whom God has gifted and called in other ways to help as well. So that means we might need to refer them out of our care when medical, psychological, or social services are needed. This is why it's important that you follow the basic guidelines for Safe Sanctuaries combined with understanding how to live them out in relationships in ministry.

**It's more than Safe Sanctuaries.** John Wesley provided the Methodist movement with many valuable insights. As we strive to create Safe Spaces, consider the following "Three Simple Rules"[14] derived from John Wesley's teaching to frame your approach to making your church's youth ministry safer for teens:

1. *Do No Harm*—This is a tough one. I am sure that along the way in my life I've done harm. I've not killed anyone or caused someone else to, so I'm pretty good, right? As ministry leaders we must ask ourselves in the process of carrying out our mission: "Are we living out this first rule?" What should we stop doing that will prevent harm and what can we start doing to prevent harm?

2. *Do Good*—Don't underestimate the power of this rule. When the disciples called Jesus "good teacher," he rebuked them and said only God is good. Having clear policies and procedures to reduce risk of harm that includes helping all in the ministry set and understand healthy boundaries will help you accomplish this rule.

3. *Stay in Love With God*—This ought to be to clear to us all, right? As you seek to reduce the risk of harm in your ministry, you are creating Safe Spaces that will become Sacred Spaces. That is our ultimate mission: creating space where all can encounter and grow more deeply in love with God.

As you have read this chapter, I hope you have gained an understanding of why we have to have to guidelines such as Safe Sanctuary policies and procedures combined with Healthy Boundaries. Just as the Old Testament gave us the Law of God, the New Testament revealed the Love of God. We need to create the sacred relationship that God desires for us. To create Safe Spaces that become Sacred Spaces, we need both Safe Sanctuaries and Healthy Boundaries to guide us and provide the framework for us to live and serve in ministry together.

# STEPHANIE'S RESPONSE

Brad has laid out an amazing soliloquy of why smaller churches must do Safe Sanctuary compliance. I've never heard anyone teach it better in a workshop than Brad.

I once heard a statistic from a big nonprofit that stated a registered sex offender attempts to join in a U.S.-based children's-focused nonprofit organization every forty-three minutes. They went on to say that the easiest to join? Small churches because "Everyone's safe here. That kind of thing doesn't happen here."

So here's my summation: Just do it. To ignore child protection guidelines is criminal itself.

# DISCUSSION QUESTIONS FOR CHAPTER 5: IT'S MORE THAN SAFE SANCTUARIES

1. What health and safety procedures are already set in place in your local church? How familiar are you with them? If you could make one change to them that you believe would make the church safer, what would it be?

2. Spend time analyzing your local church. How safe are the structure and layout? How can you restructure meeting spaces/ times in order to keep young people safe?

3. As new guests enter your church, how do they perceive the level of safety for their children and youth?

4. What personal boundaries do you have set for yourself right now? Based on this chapter, what would you like to change or add?

# CHAPTER 6

# DISCIPLESHIP

So you've built a team, you've created great job descriptions, you've equipped them for their roles, you've trained them to create Safe Spaces, and now it's game time. Creating Disciples. Sounds easy, right? If only it were as easy for us as it appeared to be for Jesus Christ! Jesus says to the young fishermen he meets, "Come, follow me, ... and I will send you out to fish for people." What was their response? "At once they left their nets and followed him" (Matthew 4:19-20, NIV).

He asked them to follow + they followed = Disciple.

A simple equation that we can replicate, right? I think we often operate like it is. However, there is more to the story. Jesus started with a personal invitation. It wasn't sent in an e-mail, listed in a worship bulletin, or hung on a cork board with all of the other fliers. It was face to face. I often wonder what was happening in the minds of Peter and Andrew as they were invited by Jesus to follow him. What was it that would cause them to drop their nets without hesitation and follow him?

## WHICH COMES FIRST?

There is debate in faith development theory about the way our belief in Jesus Christ is formed. The terms *believe*, *belong*, and *behave* are used to describe the process of faith development. The order in which they are placed is the question. Are we called to believe before we can belong? Or does belonging lead to belief? And what about behavior? Does behavior demonstrate our belief? Do we have to behave a certain way to belong? What about the invitation that starts the whole process?

## WHAT DID JESUS DO?

If we look at the Scripture from Matthew 4 when Jesus said, "Come, follow me," we see three very simple words that became an invitation to something more. Jesus didn't say to them, "After you believe I am the Son of God, come follow me." Neither did he say, "Clean up your act; then come follow me." He said, "Come, follow me." Period. As they traveled and followed, Jesus shared with them why he wanted them to follow. He told them that he saw something in them that would lead him to believe they had what it took to be a disciple. Jesus demonstrated his love for them in the way that he spoke, served, and spent time with them. In these interactions, he shared that they were now a part of a new community, a new opportunity to belong.

As he taught in the synagogues, healed the sick, and restored sight to the blind, he exhibited certain behaviors he wanted them to learn. He invited them to grow, to learn, to be transformed. He brought them into community with God the Father, Son, and Holy Spirit. As they did the things Jesus did, their belief in him grew stronger. Peter makes this revelation when Jesus asks, "Who do you say I am?" Peter answered, "You are the Messiah, the Son of the living God" (Matthew 16:15-16, NIV).

## INVITATION

That invitation was the key first step. Jesus didn't ask for a decision. He invited them to be with him. So much of our evangelism and discipleship practice is rooted more in decision than invitation. Consider the ways you've seen young people presented with the opportunity to engage in the Christian life: an open door, a great youth space, teaching, events, social media, printed material, and so on. Each one implores teens to decide, "Will I do this or not?" These methods certainly get the message out there; however, they lack the personal nature of God's invitation to be with Jesus. Further, those who never enter your church building, attend your worship services, or are not known by your congregation will likely never have the opportunity to experience the invitation.

Let's put some data to this theory. A few years ago, Lifeway Research conducted a survey of 15,000 adults. The purpose was to examine the effectiveness of different approaches to evangelism. Here are the results relating to the importance of a personal invitation:

- 67 percent of Americans say a personal invitation from a family member would be very or somewhat effective in getting them to visit a church.

- 63 percent of Americans say a personal invitation from a friend or neighbor would be very or somewhat effective in getting them to visit a church.

- 63 percent of Americans are very or somewhat willing to receive information about a local congregation or faith community from a family member.

- 56 percent of Americans are very or somewhat willing to receive information about a local congregation or faith community from a friend or neighbor.[1]

While this survey was conducted with adults, not young people, let me show you how young people operate the same way. Research conducted by the National Study of Youth and Religion revealed that parents are the single greatest influencer of their child's faith habits and behaviors.[2]

## BELONG

What drives the desire to be invited? It is an innate need for relationship and community. We were created by God to be in relationship.

Then God said, "Let us make humanity in our image to resemble us so that they may take charge of the fish of the sea, the birds in the sky, the livestock, all the earth, and all the crawling things on earth."

God created humanity in God's own image,
in the divine image God created them,
male and female God created them.

God blessed them and said to them, "Be fertile and multiply; fill the earth and master it. Take charge of the fish of the sea, the birds in the sky, and everything crawling on the ground." (Genesis 1:26-28)

God created us and invited us to be in relationship with God, each other, and creation.

Back in 2011, I had the opportunity to spend a few days with Dr. Marv Penner. Marv is a licensed marriage and family counselor specializing in parent/adolescent conflict resolution, sexual abuse recovery, eating disorders, and marriage and family issues. During the seminar, Marv talked about his book, *Help, My Kids Are Hurting.* He revealed that through his time as a youth minister and counselor he's discovered the vital role that unconditional love, belonging, and purpose play in our lives. Through his work with young people, especially those who were hurting, he found that if a person is missing one or more of those three things, turmoil ensues in his or her life and relationships. Together these three components are essential to building a lasting faith.

The first, *unconditional love,* is the kind of love that all of us desire from others. It expresses itself by giving, caring, and serving freely, compassionately, and sacrificially without expecting anything in return. The Bible calls this *agape.* It is the love that God has for us and is not dependent on our ability to return love.

The apostle Paul describes it in a way that reflects his own experience of it in Romans 5:6-8 (NIV): "You see, at just the right time, when we were still powerless, Christ died for the ungodly. Very rarely will anyone die for a righteous person, though for a good person someone might possibly dare to die. But God demonstrates his own love for us in this: While we were still sinners, Christ died for us." Empowered by the Holy Spirit, each of us as Christ followers is called to both witness to God's love and share it with those around us.

While the ways we can offer unconditional love are limitless, here is a one that is a guaranteed game changer for your young people. It can be difficult, but if you can pull it off, the sky is the limit. Ready? Listen to them. That's right. If you were expecting some new, cutting edge approach you can plug in to your program, sorry to disappoint you. When we take the time to listen to their stories without judgment and show genuine interest in the things they talk about (even if we've heard about it a million times), we offer those whom God loves the experience of God's unconditional love. This "first impression" is pivotal in their willingness to engage further in the present or return in the future. As you can imagine, it is critically important that you've helped your leadership team members—adults and teens both—understand how to listen. This can be accomplished by creating a culture where all are valued equally and all have the opportunity to be heard and at the same time learn to listen to others.

Second, *belonging* is offered to us by God, who sees us all as daughters and sons, a part of the family of God. "And I will be a father to you, and you shall be sons and daughters to me, says the Lord Almighty" (2 Corinthians 6:18, ESV). The need for belonging reveals our need for relationships with others in a community that says, "Yes, you are needed here." In the last chapter we looked at the first two of our basic needs according to Maslow. Once both the physiological needs and the need for safety are met, the next level of need is belonging. As you invite young people to join your faith community, it is essential that they experience a place where they can feel accepted.

In her book *Almost Christian,* Kenda Creasy Dean examined the data from the National Study of Youth and Religion. She identified some key characteristics of the young people who exhibited a strong faith in Christ. One essential component of building a strong faith in young people is that they have a community to belong to.[3] Young people with a deep faith were able to recognize that their congregation cared for them and could name several adults from that community who were actively influencing their faith journey. If the young people coming to your ministry don't believe they belong there, they won't stay and, what's worse, they won't hear anything you have to say about Jesus.

The third principle Marv shared is *purpose.* Everyone wants to know what their role is in this world. The existential question we all ask is, "Why am I here?" The National Study of Youth and Religion revealed that young people who exhibit a disciple-like faith realize they have a call to live out.[4] This realization that God has a purpose waiting to be discovered with the help of the Holy Spirit is essential to faith development. "But the Helper, the Holy Spirit, whom the Father will send in my name, he will teach you all things and bring to your remembrance all that I have said to you" (John 14:26, ESV). The Holy Spirit is God's way of helping direct us toward that purpose and realizing our significance. This desire for divine purpose is further driven by and connected to our longing for community. Jürgen Moltmann in his book *The Source of Life* said that this longing for community is a result of the Holy Spirit "permeat[ing] them through and through, soul and body, and bring[ing] them to a new community and fellowship with one another."[5]

## THE HAT AND SOUL

One of my ministry friends, Jerry, shared the story of one young man in the church he served.

*This young man—we'll call him Mike—showed up to youth group one night with Sarah. Sarah was the model youth group girl. She was on* the leadership council, the lead singer of the youth praise band, and a member of the church since birth. Mike, on the other hand, was different. He had never been to that church before. He had tattoos showing from under his shirt sleeves, he wore jeans that looked like they should be thrown away, and he wore a baseball hat. Mike seemed like a nice guy, though, and Sarah really seemed to like him, so Jerry didn't pay attention to Mike's appearance.

After youth group that evening, one of the older men in the church noticed Mike and immediately went to Jerry to demand that Jerry tell Mike to remove his hat. As Jerry turned to look at Mike, he and Sarah were leaving the church building.

On Sunday, Mike and Sarah came to church together once again. Mike was dressed in nicer clothes this time, but he still wore that hat. Jerry welcomed them both but didn't think to say anything about the hat. After church, once again the older man inquired what Jerry was going to do about the hat. Jerry listened and contemplated how best to talk to Mike. He didn't want the hat issue to be the thing to make Mike not come back.

Wednesday night group came and Sarah was scheduled to give the message during youth worship. Mike was there with his hat. But Jerry noticed something different about Mike. He was engaged, he was singing, he was listening to Sarah speak, and near the end of Sarah's message, Jerry could see a tear running down Mike's face. Not wanting to embarrass Mike and at the same time acknowledge his reaction, Jerry sat down next to him. During the prayer, Mike asked Jerry if they could step outside to talk. Mike began to share that he had never felt what he was feeling at that moment. He said the only reason he came to church and youth group was because he really liked Sarah. And he shared that as Sarah prepared her message this week, he was her audience as she practiced presenting it. He admitted that he hadn't really listened to the words until that night when something clicked. He said he finally realized that God did love him, that he could have a different life, and that he wanted to work on a deeper relationship with Jesus Christ.

*Jerry and Mike prayed together and returned to the group. Youth group time ended, and as Mike and Sarah left, the old guy saw Mike and his hat once more. This time angrier than before, the old guy yelled at Jerry. Why had Jerry not yet done something about the hat? In that moment while the older man was letting Jerry know just how horribly disrespectful that young man was, Jerry found these words—"I want you to know that I'm more concerned about Mike's soul than that stupid hat!"—and Jerry walked off. Mic drop!*

*It just so happened that the next morning Jerry and his wife were leaving on vacation for a week. When Jerry returned for Wednesday night group the next week, he saw Sarah walk in with a guy he didn't recognize. Just as he was about to confront Sarah for dumping Mike, Mike turned around and said hello to Jerry. Jerry hadn't recognized him because he wasn't wearing the hat anymore. Jerry, a bit concerned the old guy had gotten to Mike, asked, "What happened to the hat?" Mike, confused, replied, "Hat?" "Yeah," Jerry said, "Where's your hat? You always wear your hat." Mike replied, "That old thing? Oh, I got a haircut, so I didn't need it anymore. I was so concerned about how bad my hair looked, I thought I'd freak people out less if I wore a hat. See ya inside!"*

Jerry said he couldn't help but laugh and cry at the same time. What if Jerry had focused on the hat more than Mike's soul? The hat was inconsequential to Mike's faith journey, and Jerry realized it. Jerry's story challenges me to consider the times I might have been focused on the hat. How about you?

## BEHAVE

As young people begin to experience community, they begin to learn certain behaviors that contribute to their spiritual growth and deepening connection with others in the church. Here are some:

- reading their Bibles daily
- respect for the leader because others respect the leader
- bringing their Bibles to group meetings

- coming late to youth group because they've learned the group doesn't start on time
- sharing stories of faith with others in the group
- attending Sunday school
- giving money
- sharing stories of faith with others outside the group
- attending worship
- prayer
- raising their hands during their worship
- singing with the song leader during worship
- participating in activities
- missional service

This is not an exhaustive list, and if we're honest, there are also some negative behaviors the community would teach them that we wouldn't necessarily want them to replicate.

A caution about behavior-focused discipleship: If we're not careful, we can promote a faith that emphasizes "dos and don'ts" or morality rather than the gospel message of a redemptive relationship with Jesus Christ. The National Study of Youth and Religion found that most young people have developed a faith life that resembles a moralistic existence instead of the one displayed by the disciples. While it is good that they grow to be moral citizens, we cannot confuse culturally defined morality with following Jesus. Lack of clarity on this important distinction can lead to unintentionally nurturing a faith that is more focused on running from a hierarchical list of "sins" than predicated on running toward Jesus Christ. Behavior does matter, but as an outflow of obedience to the teachings of Jesus, not a prerequisite for belonging.

When these behaviors are displayed in your community of faith, demonstrated through role models and practiced by young people within the congregation, they serve as means of grace to help these young disciples grow in their faith. Corporate opportunities are the key. Deech Kirk, executive director of the Center for Youth

Ministry Training, warns against the tendency to separate youth and children away from congregational worship. Kirk writes:

> When we isolate youth and children's ministries from the larger church, we take away their opportunity to see mature Christian adults in action. We take away their role models. We take away their opportunity to see why faith matters to us, and how and why we worship God. . . .
>
> For the church to be in the apprenticeship business, we must place children and youth in close relationships with mature Christian adults who can show them the way.[6]

## PARENTAL INFLUENCE

Don't underestimate the important influence that parents and caregivers play in behavior formation. The National Study of Youth and Religion found that parents and congregations get the kind of faith they model. Meaning: The behaviors of the parents influence the behaviors of the child; the behaviors of the congregation influence the behaviors of the congregants. Kenda Creasy Dean says, "Teenagers' ability to imitate Christ depends, to a daunting degree, on whether *we* do."[7] Behavior matters.

Back in 1741, John Wesley didn't need a study to recognize this very situation. He gave a sermon on July 25, 1741, entitled "The Almost Christian." In it he said:

> *"Almost thou persuadest me to be a Christian."* Acts 26:28
>
> AND many there are who go thus far: ever since the Christian religion was in the world, there have been many in every age and nation who were almost persuaded to be Christians. But seeing it avails nothing before God to go *only thus far*, it highly imports us to consider,
>
> First. What is implied in being *almost,*
>
> Secondly. What in being *altogether, a Christian.*[8]

Wesley went on to talk about those who display "heathen honesty." They are good people who demonstrate a *form* of godliness. They also have an understanding of the Ten Commandments and the difference between justice and injustice. These people did the things that Christians do and refrained from those things Christian didn't do. They attended worship; they engaged in prayer and other disciplines. They had taken on the behaviors of a Christian, but they had not yet fully become "altogether Christian."

## BEHAVIOR MATTERS

So what are the behaviors that are important for forming a faith that would result in someone being declared "altogether Christian" by John Wesley or having a "consequential faith" as Kenda Creasy Dean defined in her book *Almost Christian*?

Wesley described an "altogether Christian" as possessing the following characteristics:

- Loves God passionately. One who takes seriously and strives to live Deuteronomy 6:5 (NIV): "Love the LORD your God with all your heart and with all your soul and with all your strength."

- Loves others wholeheartedly. One who exhibits an inclusive love all of people. When asked what is the greatest commandment, "Jesus replied: 'Love the Lord your God with all your heart and with all your soul and with all your mind.' This is the first and greatest commandment. And the second is like it: 'Love your neighbor as yourself.' All the Law and the Prophets hang on these two commandments" (Matthew 22:37-40, NIV).

- Has foundation faith. One who puts one's whole faith in Jesus Christ. "For I am convinced that neither death nor life, neither angels nor demons, neither the present nor the future, nor any powers, neither height nor depth, nor anything else in all creation, will be able to separate us from the love of God that is in Christ Jesus our Lord" (Romans 8:38-39, NIV).

- Faith producing repentance. A realization that Jesus Christ offers true forgiveness of sins. "'This is what is written: The Messiah will suffer and rise from the dead on the third day, and repentance for the forgiveness of sins will be preached in his name to all nations, beginning at Jerusalem" (Luke 24:46-47, NIV).

- Right and true faith. It's not just about believing the Scriptures, but it's also about having full confidence and trust in God through the work of Christ toward reconciliation with God. "It is because of him that you are in Christ Jesus, who has become for us wisdom from God— that is, our righteousness, holiness and redemption" (1 Corinthians 1:30, NIV).

In her book *Almost Christian,* Dean used the phrase "consequential faith" to describe the group of young people who exhibited the full characteristics of a follower of Christ. This group made up only 8 percent of the total group that participated in the research as part of the National Study of Youth and Religion. Examining this group further, she revealed characteristics or behaviors this group displayed that the remaining young people in the study did not.[9]

The first characteristic was that this group could articulate "a creed to believe." They were able to define the role and connection that God has in their lives. The second characteristic was that these young people knew that they had "a community to belong to." They realized that there were many adults who cared about their faith journey and were willing to engage in faith conversations with them. The third characteristic was that they had a "call to live out" in their lives, a calling that was connected to their faith in Christ for the purpose of making God's love known to the world. The fourth key behavior they displayed was the ability to articulate a "hope to hold onto," a hope for their lives that is fueled by their belief that God has a glorious plan just waiting to be revealed in a larger story.

# BELIEVE

> "Believe me: I am in my Father and my Father is in me. If you can't believe that, believe what you see—these works. The person who trusts me will not only do what I'm doing but even greater things, because I, on my way to the Father, am giving you the same work to do that I've been doing."
>
> (John 14:10-12, *THE MESSAGE*)

As we take on the behaviors of faith, we begin to internalize these behaviors as a part of who we are. As we begin to engage in consistent practice of the behaviors of Christ, those become a part of who we are. It becomes easier for us to be compassionate because not only have we learned how Jesus showed compassion but we've also experienced it and seen it modeled by those around us. As we engage in missional service, we experience the impact our actions have on those we've served as well as the impact those served have on us. And while each of these interactions and behaviors contributes to our belief, we cannot underestimate the power of the Holy Spirit at work in our lives. Early twentieth century evangelist Oswald Chambers wrote, "For the past three hundred years men have been pointing out how similar Jesus Christ's teachings are to other good teachings. We have to remember that Christianity, if it is not a supernatural miracle, is a sham."[10] Dean calls this internalization "missional imagination." It is a shifting from "self-centeredness" to "self-giving." As Dean writes, consequential faith reflects Christ who, in the words of missionary historian Andrew Walls, "sends his people as he was sent: to be the light to the world, to give healing and hope . . . , to suffer, perhaps unjustly, on behalf of others."[11]

This growing belief is enhanced by helping young people engage in art of testimony. This art is a historic practice of our Christian faith. It is a telling and retelling of the work that God is doing in and through us as we offer Jesus Christ to a hurting world. As we articulate our story of faith, we further internalize that story. It becomes more than just superficial experiences but something that is interwoven into our very being. In *Saying Is Believing: The Necessity of Testimony in Adolescent Spiritual Development,* author Amanda Hontz Drury shares: "The fullest expression of Christian living is found in the acknowledgment and articulation of where a person sees Jesus Christ at work in his or her life."[12] The practice of sharing our story of how God is at work in us is vital to the development of our belief.

The truth is, it's not just the stories we share about our faith that impact our belief. As others in our community of faith share their testimony, our stories are also reinforced. What's more is that as others share how they see God at work in our lives, our testimonies become even more defined. As I study Scripture about how Jesus interacted with the disciples and others who were present with him, I can see how stories formed their belief in who Jesus Christ is. Not only did they see him perform miraculous things but they also engaged in direct dialogue with him.

But let us not forget that even with all of the time they spent with Jesus, some still were uncertain of who he was. "Now the eleven disciples went to Galilee, to the mountain where Jesus told them to go. When they saw him, they worshipped him, but some doubted" (Matthew 28:16-17). Some doubted! That gives me hope that even those who were physically present with him doubted once in a while. Doubt is an inevitable part of the faith development process. I remember learning about and hoping that I would never be like the disciple known as Doubting Thomas. It seemed that it was almost sinful that Thomas could doubt that Jesus was who he said he was. It wasn't until just a few years ago that Thomas's perspective was explained to me in such a way that removed the stigma of doubt that my Christian education had placed on him. The pastor shared that because Thomas wasn't with the other disciples when the resurrected Jesus appeared, Thomas couldn't imagine that the same person he had witnessed crucified just a few days before would once again be alive. Thomas declared he would need to see and touch Jesus before he could believe. Thomas wanted physical proof and without it, belief would be withheld. Thomas's relationship was with the living Jesus, the one he had walked with, talked with, and seen do amazing things, but that Jesus died. For Thomas, only a physical interaction would be proof enough for him. When Jesus did show up and Thomas was able to see and touch Jesus' hands and his side, Thomas fell to his knees and said: "My Lord and my God!" (John 20:28, NIV).

I'm a lot like Thomas. And while I have not yet touched Jesus' hand, I have had the opportunity to see Jesus in action in the world. Saint Teresa of Avila was a Carmelite nun who was canonized as a Saint in the Roman Catholic Church in 1622. She is often credited with creating one of my favorite poems that reinforces for me the calling I have as a follower of Jesus Christ to make him known in the world. The poem is called "Christ Has No Body":

Christ Has No Body

Christ has no body but yours,
No hands, no feet on earth but yours,
Yours are the eyes with which he looks
Compassion on this world,
Yours are the feet with which he walks to do good,
Yours are the hands, with which he blesses all the world.
Yours are the hands, yours are the feet,
Yours are the eyes, you are his body.
Christ has no body now but yours,
No hands, no feet on earth but yours,
Yours are the eyes with which he looks
compassion on this world.
Christ has no body now on earth but yours.[13]

SMALLER CHURCH YOUTH MINISTRY

# A CHALLENGING PROCESS

In the struggle to create a welcoming community, we sometimes focus more on getting people to join us than on the reason why we want them to join us. Dietrich Bonhoeffer said, "The person who loves their dream of community will destroy community [even if their intentions are ever so earnest], but the person who loves those around them will create community."[14] Jesus invited the disciples to follow him, he welcomed them, and he started sharing the gospel. They followed him as he taught in synagogues, "proclaiming the good news of the kingdom, and healing every disease and sickness among the people" (Matthew 4:23, NIV).

The new disciples were immediately immersed in the ministry of Jesus Christ! He didn't soften the message to ensure that the new disciples would stay with him. We must resist the temptation of watering down the gospel to create belonging. Young people want to be challenged. The Growing Younger study by Fuller Youth Institute revealed that "teenagers and emerging adults in churches growing young aren't running from a gospel that requires hard things of them. They are running toward it."[15]

The reality of a broken world is presented to us daily. Poverty, war, injustice, racism, distrust, and destruction surround us regularly. Those in the current generation of young people, Generation Z, were born after 1996. They arrived after the social justice conscious Millennials and came along in the lead-up and aftermath of 9/11 and the Great Recession.[16] They don't remember a time that the United States was not at war somewhere in the world. They're smart. Researchers predict that a higher percentage of Gen Z will attend and graduate from college than previous generations. This generation is also considered the most diverse of any previous. All of these factors push Gen Z to want to make a difference in the world.[17] In his book *The Irresistible Revolution: Living As an Ordinary Radical,* Shane Claiborne says:

I am convinced that if we lose kids to the culture of drugs and materialism, of violence and war, it's because we don't dare them, not because we don't entertain them. It's because we make the gospel too easy, not because we make it too difficult. Kids want to do something heroic with their lives, which is why they play video games and join the army. But what are they to do with a church that teaches them to tiptoe through life so they can arrive safely at death?[18]

Invite them into a ministry where they can belong while challenging them to make a difference in the world. They are longing for it. The world needs a new generation of disciples of Jesus Christ who will transform the world.

# STEPHANIE'S RESPONSE

Brad has laid out in thought-provoking detail a way of discipling your young people. I've read through it twice now and it's giving me several things to chew on for what I teach and how I interact within my own home church.

So in the light of what Brad's presented, here are a few areas for you to consider in creating a discipleship path at your small church:

## 1. CREATE A PLAN

You actually have to create a plan: many churches operate as if discipleship will "just happen," and at some level, I bet it does. Some churches are more successful at it than others. But more often than not, even among churches who can check the "we got this" box of growing up solid followers of Jesus, no intentional plan exists. When I'm at churches doing assessments, I'll ask what the "teaching plan" is for the seven years a teen is in their youth ministry. Eighty-plus percent of the time, the response is, "Well, uh ... hmm."

Choosing a curriculum for Sunday school is important to being intentional about making disciples; however, it isn't enough. Finding a great new series to use at youth group isn't enough, either. To do the most you can for your students, your church has to ask this set of questions:

- What do we want our youth to know about their faith when they graduate high school?

- What do we want them to feel with their faith?

- What do we want them to do with their faith?

When wrapped up in one bundle, the answers to these questions represent the DNA of your particular church.

So after a church knows the educational competencies (the know-feel-dos) it wants to impart, it's time to look at every piece of the spiritual formation and learning puzzle in your church. In other words, the discipleship education you want for your students has to be planned in light of Sunday school, youth group, confirmation, Bible studies, summer trips, rites of passage, worship—anything where your students learn. For a solid discipleship path, each program can't operate independently of each other. Instead, they should all weave together.

Picture it like this: On a wall in front of you, there's a piece of paper, one for each of the programs or ministries where Christian education is imparted. On a table in front of you are all the subjects/topics (know-feel-dos) you want to make sure your students have a chance to learn. The next step? You start putting the sticky notes on the sheets and a plan begins to form. This is an overly simple way to picture it, but you can begin to get the idea.

When you create a plan, it keeps everyone on the same page and unplanned subject duplicity from happening. Sunday school teachers and youth group leaders work together. Pastors and youth folks collaborate for when a sermon series can back up a theme the youth need to hear. There are no renegade teachers taking the learning where the church doesn't want it to go. You get the idea.

## 2. CELEBRATE KEY MOMENTS

Look for life mile markers and memory makers. So far what I've laid out for a discipleship path can seem a little dry. It doesn't have to be! Some of *the* best discipleship moments in a student's life aren't in a class; they're learned through celebrating the life that God has given them.

Here's what I mean: Figure out a way to recognize key moments in a teen's (and his or her family's) life. Many churches do a good-to-great job at something like confirmation or some form of pastor's classes. Each May, we generally remember to honor our graduates. But what would it look like if a church figured out a way to celebrate lots of growing up moments? Each child and teenager would begin to feel like, "Hey, this church cares about me. This church is a part of my growing up. This is not just a place I visit on Sundays. This is a place that helps me live life as a teenager." Well, maybe they wouldn't use those exact words, but you get the idea.

The key: Don't just passively recognize these moments. Figure out ways that young and old can intentionally celebrate milestones together. The more opportunities a church provides for its aging population and its young people to experience community together in this way, the stronger the anchor for a young person's developing faith.

Ideas for moments to celebrate (I bet you can think of a lot more):

- When a baby learns to walk
- When a toddler goes to preschool
- From preschool to all-day school
- Loss of first tooth
- Learning to ride a bike
- From elementary school to middle school
- From middle school to high school
- Learning to drive
- Getting a driver's license
- Prom/homecoming

There's a side benefit to an intentional system of celebrating these age-level moments: it's fun! Who doesn't love a celebration? People get to know each other outside of their church inner circle. Multigenerational relationships are established; names get learned. Joy abounds. Love grows. God is glorified . . . and disciples grow.

# DISCUSSION QUESTIONS FOR CHAPTER 6: DISCIPLESHIP

1. Describe how your church invites people into your faith community. Do you find this appealing to young people? Why or why not? How can the medium of invitation be modified to be inviting to all ages?

2. In this chapter, Brad stressed the importance of belonging through the story of The Hat and Soul. How do you embrace those who may be different in your church, and how will you move toward a culture of belonging for all?

3. Kenda Creasy Dean describes in her book *Almost Christian* the four key characteristics/behaviors of youth groups. The first two were "a creed to believe" and "a community to belong to." These can be difficult to balance. How in your group would you find the balance between scriptural teachings ("serious stuff") and fellowship times ("fun stuff")?

4. How will you create a supportive environment in your church that encourages young people to use their gifts and skills in God's mission to transform the world?

# CHAPTER 7

# CRITICAL MASS

Throughout the previous chapters, I (Brad) have taken the lead and Stephanie has responded. We decided to mix it up on this chapter. When Stephanie and I first met at Simply Youth Ministry Conference in Louisville five years ago, I couldn't have imagined all that has taken place through our partnership leading the Smaller Church Youth Ministry Initiative! Stephanie has a deep passion and giftedness for equipping smaller church ministry leaders. I asked Stephanie to put some thoughts together on what it takes to build critical mass in your ministry with young people at a smaller church. My thoughts will follow.

## STEPHANIE'S THOUGHTS ON CRITICAL MASS

Common laments I hear from smaller churches:

- "But you just don't understand, Stephanie. We are just a small church."

- "We're out in the boonies. How will we ever grow?"

- "We can't have student leadership with so few kids! Every kid would be a leader!"

- "We don't have any staff. We can't 'do' youth ministry."

- "We don't have any budget. We can't 'do' youth ministry."

- "We don't have any space. We can't 'do' youth ministry."

- "We don't have any kids. We can't 'do' youth ministry."

- "We can't seem to get a critical mass of kids so that something exciting happens."

## Critical mass

*crit·i·cal mass:* noun

1. the minimum amount of fissile material needed to maintain a nuclear chain reaction
2. the minimum size or amount of resources required to start or maintain a venture[1]

Example: "A communication system is of no value unless there is a *critical mass* of users."

It's time for a moment of baseline truth: if we're talking about smaller church ministry, we're circling our wagons around the commonality of having less numbers than other churches. You know, those *big* churches down the road where ministry *must* be better, right? Brad touched upon the subject of numbers earlier on; let's camp here for a while and flesh out the subject a little bit.

- How does a small church reach the critical mass it needs for successful, sustainable ministry to happen?

- Just when do numbers matter and if our numbers need to grow—how do we do that?

- When don't the numbers matter?

Small, large, or somewhere in between—what church doesn't want loads of kids showing up at our youth events? We don't even know what number "loads" is, but whatever that number is—we know we want it and one more. We plan, prepare, program, perform, and pray; then we hope more show up than "last time."

And after your event is over, no matter how many students participated, somebody at your church is going to say something like this: "Gee. That's all? But you worked so hard. Hmmmm ... I thought there would have been more. Why won't parents make our youth events a priority? Well (like they used to say about the Cubbies), 'there's always next year.'"

So, let's unpack this critical mass thing a little, shall we?

Here are four numerical nuances in church student ministry I'd like you to consider and make mental application of in your own setting:

- When numbers are important

- When numbers don't matter a hoot

- How to determine your critical mass

- How to decrease the numbers at your youth events

## When numbers are and aren't important

When asked about their student ministry numbers, a common answer among youth workers is: "We'd rather have less students with deeper relationships than lots of students with shallow spiritual depth." Really? If that logic is the gold standard, wouldn't the correct answer be, "We'd rather have lots of students, deep into a God-relationship?"

One numbers camp leans toward "the more in attendance, the merrier!" Their mantra sounds something like this: "We had (insert some fantastic number here, sure to impress the board) come to our annual "Glow-in-the-Dark Capture-the-Flag Midnight-Manhunt" competition. Over 6,432 students heard the gospel!" The numbers reasoning behind these big events makes sense: the more arrows you shoot, the more chance of hitting the target.

Here's another viewpoint from the "but who's counting?" camp: "We have ten students solidly attending our small group Bible study. No fluff here!" They've got a point, too. A smaller student-to-leader ratio has a proven track record in planting meaningful mentorship into students.

The truth? Numbers do matter. The other truth? Numbers don't matter.

## When numbers do matter

- If you leave on a trip with twelve students, you should come home with twelve. Extra points for coming home with the same twelve.

- On Youth Sunday, it's important to have as many of your students as possible there for interacting with the larger church body. The more youth faces, the more youth funding.

- During fundraisers, more hands make your work easier and more faces make the members happy.

- When a parent says, "Why don't you ever contact my kid?," you show them your contact spreadsheet where you've kept track of each text, piece of mail, e-mail, and phone call you've made to personally invite their child. Or when the church board wonders if you're reaching out to inactive families, you can show them exactly how many and who.

Small churches who want a sustainable, thriving (notice I didn't say "large") student ministry must set target numbers goals. Those churches who gather their stakeholders and set appropriate goals for participation tend to move forward faster than those that don't. Why is that? Because when everyone knows exactly what the entire body wants to have happen, the work is more focused. Having practical game plans for how to reach students and then keeping track of the attendance at all youth ministry programming allows everyone to know how the ministry is doing in rolling toward its numbers goals. Yearly benchmarks are determined, evaluations are gathered, and adjustments are made. Everyone sets out armed with the newly tweaked game plans and all is right in the world.

Imagine it like this. Your small church wants to provide a way to show students who Jesus is and could be for them. So everyone hops on a bus (their youth ministry programming) and the bus takes off for "Youth Land"—the place where youth are. They get to where they're going, open the bus doors, and wait for students to hop on. The problem? No one decided exactly where the bus was headed and how many students they could/should gather up. They never leave the parking lot, and the bus ride is less than stellar in its results.

Back to real life. When participation goals aren't set and publicized, church members (whether connected to the youth ministry or not) will set those numbers for themselves. Conversations start popping up all over the church, grumbling and gossip arise, and the youth ministry suffers. It often sounds something like this: "We should have fifty kids in this church!" "Why, I remember when there used to be one hundred students coming every week back in my day." "We hired a youth director. Why don't we have tons of kids here?" "If we don't start getting more families with kids through these church doors, this church is going to die!"

Sound familiar? The numbers always vary. The conversations always escalate. The blame always gets placed. The youth always suffer. The youth leader always leaves.

Once the day arrives for your youth event, the number of youth who walk through the door doesn't mean a thing (except for how much pizza to order). A smart small church youth ministry is one where there's a plan for a game that can be played whether two or twelve show up. The off-property event you planned can be done with any number of kids; no minimums are needed. You and your adult volunteers are smiling and fully invested in the lives of whatever sixth- to twelfth-grader has shown up. Do you put up with an Eeyore attitude where people say stuff like, "Our poor church. Nobody loves us. Only four kids came to the new youth Bible study." Of course not! You dive in and enjoy who's there, giving those present the gift of your fully invested self, ready to share and learn together.

## When numbers don't matter

- If you plan an event and only two kids show up? Go anyway and have a great time!

- When a student needs you, only you, and there are lots of other students in the room, let your other adults take over the larger group. Don't have other adults? That's a numbers problem right there.

- When planning a killer Bible study, whether for the benefit of twenty-five youth or just one, give it all you've got! The Word never goes out without benefit. Knock 'em dead (into life)!

- School lunch dates or after-school coffee/Coke chats are great for one-on-one time. Doesn't matter how big or little your group is at that point, does it?

It's those "numbers don't matter" moments we all live for in youth ministry. Times when we're forced to slow down, take a breather, and look a student full-on in the face to ask, "So tell me what's happening, friend?" When the only number that matters is the one in front of you.

## How to increase or decrease your critical mass

On one hand, my best advice for knowing when your youth ministry meets that magical critical mass is really what I said before: you've reached it every time a student shows up for anything. Go for the gold! On the other hand, lower numbers than everyone thinks there should be could mean that something unhealthy is going on. It's the same dynamic as when we take our kids' temperature when they start to cough. If that little stick says something too far away from the 98.6 it's supposed to be, we have to make plans to nurse our wee ones back to health.

So what's a thermometer your church can use for measuring the health of your youth ministry? In my work with Ministry Architects, we've determined that ten percent of the average weekly worship attendance is a reasonable expectation level of students in your church on a weekly basis. Let me do the math for you: Your church has about eighty-five to ninety people in worship on an average week. You could reasonably expect that there be about eight or nine students who are participating somewhere within the life of your church. Wherever they've connected (Sunday school, worship only, youth group, the choir, the children's ministry, and so forth), the point is they've connected. Wherever those connection points are? That's youth ministry.

Unfortunately, not every church sends the right message that "youth ministry is welcomed and wanted here." I swear there are youth ministries out there who operate like they're purposefully trying to keep kids away. Here's a list, although not exhaustive, of dynamics that are sure to drive youth right back out your church door:

- Ignore the "celebration" days. (Neglect to remember birthdays, sports wins, awards, and so forth.)

- Forget (or never learn) their names.

- Change an event's time/location without telling *everyone!* (Showing up to an empty room is a real bummer and says to a kid, "We didn't care enough about you to give you the scoop.")

- Miss the signals they're not fitting in with the other kids.

- Neglect to notice when students are missing.

- Create your own "inner circle" and leave others standing on the outside.

- Don't care that the new kid doesn't know the "inside jokes" or stories.

- Make guests stand up and introduce themselves on their first visit. (Students don't like it any more than adults do in your service.)

- Maintain poor planning, last-minute calendaring, no data management, and poor follow-up and then find the poor ministry results are acceptable.

So how to build the numbers? Here are a few strategies I've found work well in any setting:

1. Quarterly events

2. Multigenerational moments

3. Mentorship ministry

4. Front door/back door strategies

## Quarterly events

Quarterly events still work. In a world where nothing stays the same, including in ministry, one bastion of stability has remained: vacation Bible school still works and smaller churches rise to the challenge. VBS planning and implementation bring out the best in small churches; everyone has to work together to pull it off. Look in any church kitchen during VBS week and you'll see multiple ages behind the kitchen counter ready to serve up the cookies, juice, and laughter. Older men and young guys are running around, carrying ladders and setting up backdrops. Teenage girls who wouldn't be seen with a first-grader during the school year magically transform into super teacher crew leaders with kids hanging off every limb. It's a wonderful thing; keep doing what you're doing!

Where smaller churches fall down on the VBS trail? Getting solid contact info and then having terrific follow-up. Inviting parents to an end-of-VBS event and maybe a follow-up postcard mailing aren't enough. It's the same problem with other quarterly outreach events. We plan great holiday-oriented events such as fall festival, trunk-or-treat, Bethlehem marketplaces, breakfast with Santa, Easter egg hunts, and so forth, and many churches fail to find ways to follow up with the community people attracted to these events.

My small-church friends, the gold at the end of the "grow your numbers" rainbow you're looking for is developing a quarterly events database. It's developing a system of gathering contact info from the community who comes onto your property quarterly for fun-type family events, following up with them in ways they don't feel like is spamming them, and creating a culture where they *want* to get the invite to the next big event because they felt so good after the last one.

Why? Because if you develop a solid base of people who come to your special outreach events where you show love, have fun, maybe meet a few of their personal needs while there—eventually many of these families will turn to your church for something more.

Here's an example of a quick turnaround of growth from a quarterly event: I am convinced that if you do your fall outreach event right, you'll see a direct correlation to increase attendance Christmas Eve. Think about it: Christmas Eve is the next big shot you have where the most folks will attend church. Even though many families who came to your fall festival say they have a home church, many of them really don't or they don't like the one they have. You show them the utmost of customer service and care at the fall event, they're going to think of you when it comes time to deciding on church Christmas Eve.

In my mind, a "critical mass building" fall event has the following elements. All your quarterly outreach ideas can contain similar context.

- An area with something special for the kids, where parents have to fill out contact/emergency info for participation. They wouldn't find that unusual and now you have contact info.

- An area with something special for the parents, maybe a special coffee café, where they can watch their kids, and you serve premium Pumpkin Spice concoctions. Your very best meet/greet people are working this area.

- An area where those families who need a little extra help can get it. Maybe your food bank is open or you have a winter coat giveaway. Get their contact info for needs you didn't have at the time but will follow up with them on.

- Poster boards at the exits and fliers handed out about a December event for kids and Christmas Eve info. Make sure families know there will be a nursery and a children's sermon for the kids. Don't throw in a bunch of info about all the other stuff you do for families; just appeal to the same thing that brought them to you in the first place: a fun, family, free event.

- Drawings or door prizes = cheesy way to get an e-mail address, but it works.

## Multigenerational moments

This is one of the greatest strengths a smaller church has going for it: it takes everyone to make anything happen. Since a smaller church has a smaller bandwidth for pulling off events, sprinkle the church calendar with relational times that everyone will enjoy. Ideas like the annual church talent show, New Year's Eve party with lots of areas set up for things to do, and churchwide Christmas caroling are just a few moments where you can sprinkle some intentionality in matching up your teenagers with older folks. For example, when the church goes Christmas caroling, break into assigned car teams of multi-ages where each car has something to accomplish while driving from house to house. Make it fun!

I used to serve a small church in St. Petersburg, Florida. We had an annual Pumpkin Patch to support the needs of the church. Honestly? It took everyone, all ages, to make it happen. The benefit was that lots of people of all ages who normally wouldn't spend time together did spend time together because of the work needed to run the patch. It was a relational highlight for our little church, and attendance on Sundays was never better. Plus, we had a fall festival in the midst of it, built community relationship, sold more pumpkins, collected a few more children and youth for our weekly ministry, and . . . you get the idea.

## Mentorship ministry

Nothing new here in this idea, but I don't think enough small churches try it and they should. When a church has less than a handful of youth and can't always pull off a youth group, partnering each student with an adult in the church is a way to still make successful relational ministry happen. Don't just make the program an "each pairing does their own thing." Give it some developmental Christian formation goals. I've seen successful mentoring programs based on a discipleship process, on apprenticeship within church ministries, or a prayer partners system.

## Front door/back door strategies

It is so important that every youth ministry, no matter the size (but especially one trying to build up its critical mass), has a solid first-time guest experience plan with productive follow-up. I bet you're thinking, "We don't ever have any new kids come." Well, when you do, are you ready? Because if you aren't, you won't get many chances at any other first-timers. Here's a list to consider:

- Train your students to know what to do when someone new comes.

- Train your students to know what to do when they bring someone new.

- Look at your entire youth experience through the eyes of a newcomer:

    —Is it easy to find the door to come in?

    —Is there someone at the door checking people in (another way to get up-to-date contact info) and greeting everyone?

—Are there signs leading to the youth area?

—Is there someone who will show the new person where the bathrooms are, explain the group's traditions, make introductions?

- Have several people lined up to let the first-timer know this visit was appreciated. This should include the youth leader, the pastor, and one or two youths from the group.

Equally important, if you don't want to lose what precious number of students you have, make sure you're keeping track of who is and who isn't coming. Tracking should include youth group, Sunday school, worship, confirmation, and any other regular program where students are present. Set a determined number of weeks a student turns up MIA, and then have a default plan kick into place. At minimum, it's a phone call from the leaders. At best, there are multiple people checking on the absent student. If you discover there's a need to be met or a problem to solve, then you do it and quickly. Anything after three weeks is too long to go without checking up on someone. More than that and the student in question will have created other habits and attending church isn't one of them.

Let's close with a few more critical numbers:

- There are 168 hours in a week.

- The average church kid spends about 45 minutes a week at church stuff.

- Active church attendance in America is now considered one time a month.

An old adage: Counting numbers doesn't matter if students don't feel like they count.

Now let's get out there and each one reach one.

# BRAD'S RESPONSE

Way back in Chapter 1, I introduced you to the concepts of the Small Church versus Smaller Church Mentality. This is exactly what Stephanie is talking about in this chapter. She nailed it. Here's a chart comparing the two ways of thinking that summarizes the shift we want cohort churches to make:

| Small Church Mentality | Small(er) Church Mentality |
|---|---|
| Says: We can't _____ because we're small | Says: Because we're smaller, we can _____ |
| Pastor-centered ministry | Pastor equips and empowers others for ministry |
| Hero-leader focused | Team-focused |
| Numbers-focused | People-focused |
| Lacks a calendar for the ministry | Prepares a fifteen- to eighteen-month calendar |
| Fear of change | Embraces change |
| Hopes discipleship formation happens | Plans for discipleship formation |
| Prepares for decline | Prepares for growth |

From reading this book, you might get the impression that every church that participated in the Smaller Church Youth Ministry Initiative experienced the same transformation toward building sustainable systems and structures. I don't want to mislead you because that's not the case.

The reality is that those churches who committed to implementing the training content, engaged fully in the coaching process, and did the hard work of building the teams and systems did see transformation. But there were some who didn't. Some of the churches in the cohort experienced instability in leadership during the process. Some experienced a lack of commitment to the process. And others didn't trust the process enough to take advantage of the learning from the training and coaching sessions. While these outcomes were disappointing, there is still opportunity for each of those churches to build something sustainable. It's never too late to make the effort.

## WHAT IT TAKES

The move toward building critical mass doesn't have to be a massive leap. Just commit to adding one new process that Stephanie spelled out in this chapter. For most of us, that first step might be to create a database of all of the young people on the church roster. What if your church doesn't have a roster? Start one. Before this week's worship service, take a moment and create a simple form that each attendee will complete; be sure to ask for family members' names, ages, and birthdays. Create some extra copies for the next week's service for the new folks to fill out. After you collect them, begin to create a database. We recommend that churches in the cohort use Google Sheets. Google has some great tools that are free to use online. Once this database is created, you can share it with others in leadership at your church. Some great tutorial videos on *YouTube.com* show you how.

After you take the first step, then take another. Allow each new step to be the launching point toward building critical mass. One of my favorite movies from my childhood (it still is) is the 1970 animated classic *Santa Claus Is Comin' to Town.* I love the part of the movie when Kris meets Winter. Winter tells Kris that he's really a mean and despicable creature at heart. Winter doesn't believe he can be anything different. But Kris tells him, "Changing from bad to good's as easy as taking your first step." And they break into song singing about making progress one step at a time. Check out the song by searching online for "Put One Foot in Front of the Other."

My hope for you is that you take the first step and put one foot in front of the other so you'll begin building a sustainable ministry through which God will "do immeasurably more than all we ask or imagine, according to his power that is at work within us, to him be glory in the church and in Christ Jesus throughout all generations, for ever and ever! Amen" (Ephesians 3:20-21, NIV).

# DISCUSSION QUESTIONS FOR CHAPTER 7: CRITICAL MASS

1. Reflect on how your church views numbers. Are they important? Why or why not? What one idea from this chapter can help your church begin to have a healthy attitude about numbers?

2. Brainstorm what a mentorship program might look like in your church. Whom would you recruit from your congregation? Your community? How can you use this program to gain a better critical mass?

3. From the chart shared in Brad's response, identify a couple of different ways of thinking you've heard expressed (or even expressed yourself) from the Small Church Mentality column. How might the leadership of both the church and youth ministry help the congregation embrace thinking described in the Small(er) Church Mentality column?

# CHAPTER 8

# 50 QUICK TIPS

Stephanie and I wanted to mix it up a bit with this last chapter as well, so we asked the coaching team for the Smaller Church Youth Ministry Initiative to share some tips for smaller church youth ministry. We've narrowed their input down to 50 tips. You don't have to use them all. Pick a few to start. Experiment and have fun with them.

1. **Be YOU!** You are the only version of you in the world. Be authentic. The young people in your ministry want to know you rather than a copy of someone else.

2. **Find mentors, coaches, and prayer partners for yourself.** Not only do you need a community, but you also need those people you can call who will be honest with you. You want these people to be those who know you well. They may not necessarily be ministry folks, but they can offer wisdom from a wealth of life experience. There are some great organizations such as Ministry Architects and The Youth Cartel that can provide ministry coaching if you desire a focused experience.

3. **Be connectional—share and receive ideas from other youth workers.** In addition to the group of people mentioned in No. 2, you also need a community of

colleagues—other youth workers—to share joys, concerns, and ideas. If none exist in your area, start one. Some great groups are formed on social media as well.

4. **Spend time daily in the Bible.** A pot that's empty pours no water. If you've already read the translation you have, borrow or buy a new translation. There are literally hundreds of different translations available.

5. **Let your yes be yes and your no be no.** If you say yes to something, follow through. If you say no to something, follow through. If you're unsure when to say yes and when to say no, hold off giving an answer until you've had time to think it through. For more on this, check out the information on Personal Vocational Values in Chapter 5.

6. **Join a covenant group.** Pull some friends together for coffee and talk about life and Jesus. If schedules don't permit face-to-face meetings, then pour yourself a cup and jump on Google Hangout with them.

7. **Be a risk taker; don't be afraid of failure.** You know the old adage, "It's better to have tried and failed than to not have tried at all." Take calculated risks and try new methods. Don't take risks on student and leader safety.

8. **Learn to say, "I don't know. Let's discover it together."** You don't have to have all of the answers. Learn to help facilitate discovery rather than provide answers.

9. **Learn to accept compliments and see what others see in you.** You are your worst critic. Be kind to yourself. Accept praise. Know you are loved.

10. **Create your circle of eight.** Create a list of the eight people whose opinions you value the most. When you face criticism, share it with the eight, and listen to their feedback. Respond appropriately.

11. **Never wrestle with a pig; you'll get dirty and the pig will love it.** Not every situation requires a response. Be honest. Be direct. Be compassionate. But stay out of the dirt.

12. **Own your mistakes.** If you messed up, own it. Don't blame others. Be the first to offer a solution and the first to offer an apology. Then forgive yourself and move forward.

13. **Don't be the church down the street.** Spend time discovering the uniqueness of your congregation. Don't try to compete with or compare your ministry to others in the community.

14. **Make prayer a priority.** Saturate your entire ministry in prayer. This is the most valuable thing you can do for your ministry. Create a prayer team. Invite the oldest Sunday school class in your church to pray for the ministry every day.

15. **Find opportunities for intergenerational ministry.** Your church is multigenerational, but that's not the same as intergenerational ministry. Intergenerational ministry happens when young people and older people actually study God's Word together, serve together, and enjoy relationship with one another.

16. **Jesus was relationship focused.** Measure your success by the relationships, not by the numbers.

17. **Stay on the Jesus train.** There are lots of things that can steal your focus in ministry. Keep your focus on growing in the love and knowledge of Jesus and learn from him about doing ministry.

18. **Build teams for ministry.** Don't be a hero-leader! Use the information in this book to build your team.

19. **When recruiting your team, personally ask them to serve.** Be specific, give them a job description, a timeline, and a retirement plan.

20. **Help others shine!** Put people in the places on the team where they can utilize their gifts the most. Set them up for success from the start.

21. **You have more volunteers waiting to serve than you think.** Don't get stuck in the muck of thinking you don't have enough people to serve in ministry. You might need to change your criteria of what a youth minister looks like.

22. **Look for opportunities to praise your team.** Practice saying these three words: I appreciate you! Now practice saying these two words: Thank you. Say it often. Say it unsolicited. Say it without expectation. Now go and praise your team!

23. **Have fun and build trust.** Spend time with your team outside of regular ministry meetings to have fun and build trust.

24. **No gatekeepers needed.** Create a culture for your team members that they should be involved with the young people in the ministry, not guarding the door.

25. **A few blessed subtractions. Sometimes you might have to ask volunteers to take a break from serving.** Don't be afraid. Do it with honesty. Do it with grace. Offer forgiveness. Move forward.

26. **Keep your pastor informed.** It's never a good thing for your church pastor to be surprised about something that happened in the ministry. Be the first to inform.

27. **Communicate. Communicate. Communicate.** Did we say communicate? You can never communicate enough. Some marketing researchers say people need to be exposed to information as many as twenty times before they respond to it.

28. **Invest in a wall calendar.** Keep the calendar updated with all of the activities the ministry has planned. This means you'll need to spend time planning the calendar. We suggest that you plan fifteen to eighteen months ahead.

29. **Get organized.** If this is not a skill you have, ask for help from someone in your congregation who does. We also recommend this PDF resource on the "Rhythmic Week": *tinyurl.com/zjt8sod* (that's the shortened link to *yma.wpengine.com/wp-content/uploads/2015/03/ Rhythmic-Week-AKA-Slot-System-Template.pdf*).

30. **Practice Sabbath.** Determine a regular time during the week that you will set aside to disconnect from work, technology, social media, phone calls, and so forth. Use the Rhythmic Week template above to help set your work and Sabbath schedule.

31. **Partner with other churches.** Don't be afraid to partner with other churches in your community. The reality is, your young people already know their young people. Share resources, training opportunities, mission trips, and special events.

32. **Allow young people opportunity to lead.** Your church can be the most dynamic leadership development opportunity for young people in your community.

33. **Ask young people if God is calling them to vocational ministry.** You'll recognize them, but you still need to ask. Your words might be the message that they were waiting to hear.

34. **When you ask someone to take the lead, let them.** Asking someone to lead but then taking over that responsibility is harmful to them and the team. Trust them; give support as needed.

35. **Dream big enough that God has to be in charge of it happening.** Most of our dreams are too small. We scale our dreams to meet our capabilities rather than God's. Read Ephesians 3:20 and then dream.

36. **Become a storyteller.** Learn how to tell the story of the ministry. Everyone loves a well-told story of how God is at work. Invite the congregation into the story.

37. **Respond.** There are not many things that upset parents and pastors more than lack of response. When asked a question through e-mail or text, don't forget to respond. If you're unsure of the answer, respond that you'll research the solution and then reply later.

38. **Don't be afraid to talk about the tough stuff.** Create opportunities to talk about the tough topics and questions that young people have. Make an "Ask the Tough Stuff" drop box where young people can write out their questions. Then spend some time with your team reviewing the questions and determine how best to discuss them with the group.

39. **Learn to listen more than you speak.** If you are like most ministry leaders, we like to talk. Become an observer. Become a listener. Respond when necessary.

40. **Be present.** We can be absent emotionally and mentally while physically present. With all of the ways we have to connect with each other, the most important is emotional and mental presence. Put another way, be actively engaged. Resist the temptation of checking your phone, your e-mail, or your social media accounts when meeting with people.

41. **Don't isolate yourself.** It can be easy to become myopically focused on the ministry you're leading. Be

involved in other ministries in your congregation. Partner with the children's ministry, the missions ministry, the adult discipleship groups, and others.

42. **Read and repeat.** There are a lot of great books on building ministry with young people. Pick one, spend time reading it, highlight the important stuff, write in the margins, discuss it with your mentor and your team. Implement what you can. Repeat.

43. **Be prepared.** You will get what you give. Study the lesson at least three days before the session. Anticipate challenges. Be creative. Prior planning prevents poor performance.

44. **Parents are important.** Parents are an important audience. Spend time building their trust. Communicate with parents as much as or more than you do with their children.

45. **Stick to it.** When you try something new, stick to it. Just because it wasn't successful the first time you tried it doesn't mean it was the wrong thing. Assess what needs to be different and improve. Constant change creates instability and uncertainty.

46. **Enough is enough.** Sometimes, it's time. Know when to make changes and commit to them.

47. **Seek help, ask questions.** Don't be afraid to ask questions when you don't know the answers. When you seek help to discover solutions, you're inviting others to partner with you.

48. **Celebrate.** Throw a party. Have fun. Celebrate successes.

49. **Check the facts.** Before sending out communication about the ministry, check the facts to make sure the message is well-written and has complete information. Remember to include the who, what, where, when, how much, and how transportation will be handled.

50. **Always ask: Who is not yet with us?** One of the best messages I have ever read (outside of the Bible, of course) was given by Dr. Rowan Williams, Archbishop of Canterbury, in 2012 to the World Council of Churches. He said, "Unity is neither a means nor an end. Unity is what God has given us in the church." He said the responsibility of Christians who receive the gift of unity lies in "seeking a life in which no one is without the other." This life, "constantly moving us forward into a further truth," compels all who live within the love of God to ask the question: "Who is not yet here?"[1] When we ask, "Who is not yet here?," it reminds us that Christ calls us to "go and make disciples of all nations, baptizing them in the name of the Father and of the Son and of the Holy Spirit" (Matthew 28:19, NIV).

## DISCUSSION QUESTIONS FOR CHAPTER 8: 50 QUICK TIPS

1. Which three of these tips do you struggle with the most?

2. How can you shift these into strengths, for both yourself and your overall team?

# NOTES

## Notes on Chapter 1: The Power of Small(er)

1. From "Fast Facts about American Religion," Hartford Seminary's Hartford Institute for Religion Research website, *tinyurl.com/ormjvh.* Accessed 30 June 2016.
2. From "Fast Facts about American Religion."
3. From *The Book of Discipline of The United Methodist Church—2012.* Copyright © 2012 by The United Methodist Publishing House; ¶ 201, page 143. Used by permission. All rights reserved.
4. From "Fast Facts about American Religion."
5. From "Data Services," The United Methodist Church website, *tinyurl.com/jc9gkng.* Accessed 30 June 2016.
6. From *Cultural Anthropology,* 2nd ed., by Paul G. Hiebert (Grand Rapids, Michigan: Baker Book House, 1976), page xxi.
7. From Hiebert, page xxi.
8. From *Renew Your Congregation: Healing the Sick, Raising the Dead,* by William T. McConnell (Chalice Press, 2007), page 17.

## Notes on Chapter 2: What If...?

1. From *Systematic Theology, Volume 2: Existence and the Christ,* paperback ed., by Paul Tillich (The University of Chicago Press, 1975), page 116.
2. From "How Youth Doubt is Different Than We Expected," by Andrew Zirschky, 19 February 2014, Center for Youth Ministry Training website, *tinyurl.com/z7gku8g,* as quoted in "Four Words That Can Transform Your Conversations With Teenagers," by Brad M. Griffin, 6 April 2014, Fuller Youth Institute website, *tinyurl.com/zr9jwuc.* Both accessed 6 July 2016.

## Notes on Chapter 3: Building

1. From "Abe Reichental quotes," ThinkExist.com Quotations website, *thinkexist.com/quotes/abe_reichental*. Accessed 13 July 2016.
2. From *Start With Why: How Great Leaders Inspire Everyone to Take Action,* by Simon Sinek (New York: Penguin Group, 2009), page 45.
3. From *Sustainable Youth Ministry: Why Most Youth Ministry Doesn't Last and What Your Church Can Do About It,* by Mark DeVries (Downers Grove, Illinois: InterVarsity Press, 2008), pages 55–56.
4. DeVries, page 37.

## Notes on Chapter 4: Leading

1. From "Jesus' Disciples: A Teenage Posse?," by Kay Bonikowsky, 20 August 2008, in *The Happy Surprise* blog, *tinyurl.com/z7ngap8*. Accessed 20 September 2016.
2. From "History," Howard Thurman Center for Common Ground website, *bu.edu/thurman/about/history*. Accessed 21 September 2016.
3. From "Gradual Release of Responsibility: I Do, We Do, You Do" (PDF), San Juan Board of Cooperative Educational Services website, *sjboces.org/doc/Gifted/GradualReleaseResponsibilityJan08.pdf*. Accessed 22 September 2016.
4. From "What Do Young People Really Want in a Church?," by Jake Mulder, 1 August 2016, Fuller Youth Institute website, *tinyurl.com/jj9f634*. Accessed 19 September 2016.
5. Gavin Richardson's writings can be found at the YouthWorker Circuit website, *youthworkercircuit.com*. Accessed 26 September 2016.
6. From "Projections of the Size and Composition of the U.S. Population: 2014 to 2060" (PDF), by Sandra L. Colby and Jennifer M. Ortman, March 2015, page 4, United States Census Bureau website, *tinyurl.com/ohxe279*. Accessed 26 September 2016.

## Notes on Chapter 5: It's More Than Safe Sanctuaries

1. From "Safe Sanctuaries," Disciples Ministries of The United Methodist Church website, *umcdiscipleship.org/leadership-resources/safe-sanctuaries*. Accessed 26 September 2016.
2. From "Child Sexual Abuse Statistics," National Center for Victims of Crime website, *victimsofcrime.org/media/reporting-on-child-sexual-abuse/child-sexual-abuse-statistics*. Accessed 26 September 2016.
3. From "Child Sexual Abuse Statistics."
4. From "The Abel and Harlow Child Molestation Prevention Study" (PDF), page 7, excerpted from *The Stop Child Molestation Book,* by Gene G. Abel and Nora Harlow (Xlibris, 2001), *childmolestationprevention.org/pdfs/study.pdf*. Accessed 26 September 2016.

5. From "Startling Statistics: Child Sexual Abuse and What the Church Can Begin Doing About It," by Boz Tchividjian, 9 January 2014, Religion News Service website, *religionnews.com/2014/01/09/startling-statistics*. Ellipsis is present in the article. Accessed 26 September 2016.
6. From "Maslow's Hierarchy of Needs," by Saul McLeod, 2007, updated 2016, SimplyPsychology website, *simplypsychology.org/maslow.html*. Accessed 27 September 2016.
7. From "Many Churches Neglect to Screen Those Working with Children and Youth," 6 November 2007, Barna Group website, *tinyurl.com/zhpxw78*. Accessed 27 September 2016.
8. From *Safe Sanctuaries for Youth: Reducing the Risk of Abuse in Youth Ministries,* by Joy Thornburg Melton (Nashville: Discipleship Resources, 2004), page 27.
9. From "Tip Sheet: Child Sexual Abuse Prevention for Faith Communities," Stop It Now! website, *stopitnow.org/ohc-content/tip-sheet-10*. Accessed 27 September 2016.
10. From Melton, page 8.
11. From "Teens, Social Media & Technology Overview 2015: 73% of Teens Have Access to a Smartphone; 15% Have Only a Basic Phone," 8 April 2015, Pew Research Center website, *tinyurl.com/zrqa9b6*. Accessed 28 September 2016.
12. From "#NoFilter: Parenting Teens on Social Media," by Kevin Alton, 28 April 2016, Institute for Youth Ministry at Princeton Theological Seminary website, *iym.ptsem.edu/category/social-media*. Ellipses are present in the article. Accessed 28 September 2016.
13. From "Jesus Set Boundaries," by Bill Gaultiere, 20 July 1998, Soul Shepherding website, *soulshepherding.org/1998/07/jesus-set-boundaries*. Accessed 28 September 2016.
14. An interpretation of John Wesley's three general rules is given in the book *Three Simple Rules: A Wesleyan Way of Living,* by Rueben P. Job (Nashville: Abingdon Press, 2007).

## Notes on Chapter 6: Discipleship
1. From "Strategic Evangelism: The Power of an Invitation," by Ed Stetzer, 21 July 2014, in *The Exchange: A Blog* by Ed Stetzer, *tinyurl.com/qx2fkoj*. Accessed 19 September 2014.
2. From "Research Findings," National Study of Youth & Religion website, *youthandreligion.nd.edu/research-findings*. Accessed 19 September 2016.
3. From *Almost Christian: What the Faith of Our Teenagers Is Telling the American Church,* by Kenda Creasy Dean (New York: Oxford University Press, 2010), page 49.
4. From Dean, page 49.

5. From *The Source of Life: The Holy Spirit and the Theology of Life,* by Jürgen Moltmann, translated by Margaret Kohl (London: SCM Press, 1997), page 104.
6. From "Congregations As Families of Faith: Beyond Age-Level Ministries," by Deech Kirk, 16 April 2013, Ministry Matters website, *tinyurl.com/hcxqraf.* Accessed 19 September 2016.
7. From Dean, page 112.
8. From Sermon 2, "The Almost Christian," by John Wesley, in *The Sermons of John Wesley,* ed. Thomas Jackson, Global Ministries of the United Methodist Church website, *tinyurl.com/hunq8pa.* Accessed 19 September 2016.
9. From Dean, pages 40–42.
10. From *The Complete Works of Oswald Chambers* (Grand Rapids, Michigan: Discovery House Publishers, 2000), page 548.
11. From Dean, page 84.
12. From *Saying Is Believing: The Necessity of Testimony in Adolescent Spiritual Development,* by Amanda Hontz Drury (Downers Grove, Illinois: InterVarsity Press, 2015), page 64.
13. "Christ Has No Body," by Teresa of Avila (attributed), "Poetry Selections," Journey With Jesus website, *tinyurl.com/yzhzxql.* Accessed 20 September 2016.
14. From *The Irresistible Revolution: Living As an Ordinary Radical,* by Shane Claiborne (Grand Rapids, Michigan: Zondervan, 2006), page 320.
15. From "What Do Young People Really Want in a Church?," by Jake Mulder, 1 August 2016, Fuller Youth Institute website, *tinyurl.com/jj9f634.* Accessed 19 September 2016.
16. From "Move Over, Millennials, Here Comes Generation Z," by Alex Williams, 18 September 2015, *The New York Times* website, *tinyurl.com/holoqwr.* Accessed 19 September 2016.
17. From "Top 10 Gen Z and iGen Questions Answered," The Center for Generational Kinetics website, *tinyurl.com/hnw65j5.* Accessed 20 September 2016.
18. From Claiborne, page 226.

## Notes on Chapter 7: Critical Mass

1. From entry on "critical mass," *Oxford Dictionary of Phrase and Fable,* edited by Elizabeth Knowles (New York: Oxford University Press, 2006).

## Notes on Chapter 8: 50 Quick Tips

1. From "Unity Is God's Gift to the Church, Says Archbishop of Canterbury," 28 February 2012, World Council of Churches website, *tinyurl.com/hrkjyg7.* Accessed 21 September 2016.

# APPENDIX

# IT'S MORE THAN SAFE SANCTUARIES RESOURCES

## WEBSITES

• *NetSmartz.org*
This is a cyber safety site offered by the National Center for Missing and Exploited Children.

• *tnumc.org/safe-spaces-ministry*
This is the website resource page for the Safe Spaces Ministry of the Tennessee Conference of The United Methodist Church. New resources are added regularly.

• *umcdiscipleship.org/leadership-resources/safe-sanctuaries*
This website is the resource site for The United Methodist Discipleship Ministry: Safe Sanctuaries.

## BOOKS

• *Safe Sanctuaries: Reducing the Risk of Abuse in the Church for Children and Youth,* by Joy Thornburg Melton. Available through *cokesbury.com*

Description (provided by Cokesbury): This ten-year anniversary edition of the bestselling *Safe Sanctuaries* series brings together—in one volume—the transformative and foundational information found in Joy Thornburg Melton's previous two volumes. *Safe Sanctuaries* remains the only resource of its kind that offers the tools necessary to train leaders of the church to keep the children and youth safe. This volume is updated to include information on the growing concern around the Internet and predators as well as a new section on vulnerable adults.

• *CyberSafety for Families Training Kit* (CD), by Paul O'Briant. Available through *cokesbury.com*

Description (provided by Cokesbury): Worried about the safety of children on the Internet? The CyberSafety for Families CD is designed to help you, whether you are a parent, children's or youth minister, or church leader. It offers tips for talking with children about cybersafety, establishing family guidelines for using the Internet, teaching plans, and all the tools you need for a presentation to your church community. A perfect tool to educate yourself, parents, or your church community. The CD includes step-by-step teaching plans, masters for handouts (including guidelines for talking to children about Internet bullying, setting family guidelines for use of the Internet), a PowerPoint slideshow and script, an audio recording, and much more.

• *Cyber-Safe Kids, Cyber-Savvy Teens: Helping Young People Learn to Use the Internet Safely and Responsibly,* by Nancy Willard. Available through *cokesbury.com*

Description (provided by Cokesbury): Essential strategies to keep children and teens safe online. As our children and teens race down the onramp to the Information Superhighway, many parents feel left behind in the dust. News stories about online sexual predators, child pornography, cyber bullies, hate groups, gaming addiction, and other dangers that lurk in the online world make us feel increasingly concerned about what our children are doing (and with whom) in cyberspace. In *Cyber-Safe Kids, Cyber-Savvy Teens,* Internet safety expert Nancy Willard provides you with need-to-know information about those online dangers, and she gives you the practical parenting strategies necessary to help children and teens learn to use the Internet safely and responsibly. Parents protect younger children by keeping them in safe places, teaching them simple safety rules, and paying close attention. As children grow, we help them gain the knowledge, skills, and values to make good choices—choices that will keep them safe and show respect for the rights of others. In *Cyber-Safe Kids, Cyber-Savvy Teens,* Willard shows you how those same strategies can be translated from the real world to the cyberworld, and that you don't have to learn advanced computer skills to put them into effect. As you work on these strategies with your child, you will also discover that remaining engaged with what your children are doing online is much more valuable than any blocking software you could buy.

• *A Parent's Guide to Understanding Social Media: Helping Your Teenager Navigate Life Online,* by Mark Oestreicher and Adam McLane. Available through *theyouthcartel.com/ product/a-parents-guide-to-understanding-social-media*

Description (provided by The Youth Cartel): With each passing day, teenagers' lives become increasingly intertwined with social media. How can you as a parent stay informed and involved in healthy ways? How can you help your son or daughter make wise decisions and remain safe online? *A Parent's Guide to Understanding Social Media* will equip you to have meaningful conversations with your teenager about the best, wisest ways to get connected while staying safe. Your guides for this journey are Mark Oestreicher and Adam McLane, who draw from their own wells of experience as parents and youth workers. They'll help you chart a course toward discovering and practicing wise family online activity.

• *Right Click: Parenting Your Teenager In A Digital Media World (A Sticky Faith Guide),* by Art Bamford, Kara Powell, and Brad M. Griffin. Available through *fulleryouthinstitute.org/store/ item/right-click*

Description (provided by Fuller Youth Institute): Feel like your kids are drowning in a sea of new questions, apps, and devices? Want to talk about digital media more with your kids, but aren't sure how?

Help is here. *Right Click* helps you think and talk differently about digital media, as you learn from inspiring and creative parents like you who navigate these ever-changing waters day after day. Approach this new connected world like a team and address your most pressing tech-related dilemmas. How do I teach my kids to use social media responsibly? Why do my kids constantly check their phones? How can we be present when we're in the same room? How do I handle the tough stuff: inappropriate sharing, bullying, and porn? How do I make digital media a force that knits our family together rather than ripping us apart?

CPSIA information can be obtained
at www.ICGtesting.com
Printed in the USA
LVOW08s1002041116
511420LV00008BA/17/P